MW00440005

FINANCIAL
OVER
FLOW

10 BIBLE PRINCIPLES TO UNLOCK
HEAVEN'S UNENDING SUPPLY

JONATHAN D. SHUTTLESWORTH

FINANCIAL
OVER
FLOW

FINANCIAL OVERFLOW

10 BIBLE PRINCIPLES TO UNLOCK HEAVEN'S UNENDING SUPPLY

Jonathan D. Shuttlesworth

Financial Overflow
10 Bible Principles to Unlock Heaven's Unending Supply
By Jonathan D. Shuttlesworth

Copyright © 2017 by Revival Today

Unless otherwise indicated, all Scripture quotations are taken from the *New Living Translation* of the Bible.

Published by Revival Today Publishing

Revival Today
P.O. Box 254
Oakdale, PA 15071
412-787-2578
Website: www.revivaltoday.com

ISBN: 978-0-9981753-1-7

Dedication

I dedicate this book to my Lord, Savior and Master, Jesus Christ. Fifteen years ago, I began serving you in the ministry and haven't been to the hospital since. I've never lacked. I've been kept safe in the air, on the road, and at sea. You are not a liar. You are a covenant keeping God. Every blessing I have is from your sacrifice. Thank you for the matchless privilege of serving you. I owe a debt of love I can never repay.

I would also like to thank my parents, Tiff and Judy Shuttlesworth. How invaluable to have a soul-winning father and mother who taught me to live holy and disregard any opinion contrary to God's Word. I love you!

CONTENTS

Introduction

I am writing this book to you, the man or woman holding it in their hands. I believe God has a great part for you to play in this final worldwide revival.

It's terrible to not see your dreams come true. It's heartbreaking to have a God-given vision in your spirit and lack the resources to bring it to pass. If you've ever struggled with similar thoughts before, this book is for you! These 10 principles from God's Word, when acted upon, will put an end to your frustration and bring you the greatest joy there is – fulfilling God's plan for your life.

This book is important. Proverbs teaches us that the rich rule over the poor. The nations are in turmoil because laws are being written by those who want to promote sin and silence the voice of the Church. It's not the will of God for evil men to rule over the righteous. I'm writing this to you, in faith, that you're a part of an end-time generation of Abrahams. A Christian who is not content to see your nation destroyed. A Christian, who will rise up in the power of God, and possess the gates of the enemy.

I'd be remiss if I failed to acknowledge the debt I owe to those who've impacted my life. I am forever indebted to Bishop David Oyedepo and the impact his preaching has made on my life. Any copying of his phrasing or thoughts is unintentional, but unavoidable. Thank you for serving our generation and for the immeasurable grace of God upon your life.

Chapter 1

Breaking a Poverty Mentality

"No one can serve two masters. For you will hate one and love the other; you will be devoted to one and despise the other. You cannot serve both God and money. That is why I tell you not to worry about everyday life – whether you have enough food and drink, or enough clothes to wear. Isn't life more than food, and your body more than clothing? Look at the birds. They don't plant or harvest or store food in barns, for your heavenly Father feeds them. And aren't you far more valuable to him than they are? Can all your worries add a single moment to your life? And why worry about your clothing? Look at the lilies of the field and how they grow. They don't work or make their clothing, yet Solomon in all his glory was not dressed as beautifully as they are. And if God cares so wonderfully for wildflowers that are here today and thrown into the fire tomorrow, he will certainly care for you. Why do you have so little faith?"

MATTHEW 6:24-30

Jesus uses this section of Scripture in Matthew, to break a poverty mentality in people. Instructing them not to worry about what they will eat or wear. As a Christian, your life shouldn't be consumed with these worries. This is what the

1

heathen thinks and focuses on. You will never reach abundance with a poverty mindset. I once heard Bishop David Oyedepo say, "If it's too big for your mouth, it's too big for your hands." Meaning, if you don't speak prosperity, you'll never have prosperity.

Many ministries that are ashamed to preach publically on prosperity will tell you privately, "I believe in prosperity but I just don't say it from the pulpit." Thus, they never partake in prosperity. For until you believe it in your heart, think it with your mind, and speak it with your mouth, you can't have it. If you're ashamed to say it, you'll never have it. Likewise, if you believe in healing privately, but are ashamed to declare it publically, you're never going to receive healing.

The Bible says *real* faith is *speaking* faith. 2 Corinthians 4:13 says, **"But we continue to preach because we have the same kind of faith the psalmist had when he said, 'I believed in God, so I spoke.'"** If nothing flows from your heart that causes you to speak it, then you're never going to receive it.

Bishop David Oyedepo shares the story of a woman that worked in his church back when it was very small and he was extremely poor. He had started preaching on prosperity from the revelation he received by reading Kenneth and Gloria Copeland's books. One day the woman that worked for him came to his office on the verge of tears and said, "Bishop, the things people say about you in town, I can't bear it anymore. Please stop saying that you are going to be rich." He replied, "No, I'm not saying that I'm going to be rich. I'm saying that I am going to be the richest of the rich." Even back then, third-world broke; he caught a revelation of prosperity, began to speak it, and is now personally worth over $150 million dollars. All the while, remaining scandal-free. Remember, if it's too big for your mouth, it's too big for your hand. You can give and do all you want, but it's useless if your words are constantly defeating your actions.

The Bible says, **"Death and life are in the power of the tongue: and they that love it shall eat the fruit thereof"** (Proverbs 18:21, KJV). If you are speaking death, you can actually cancel out your giving. Plenty of people speak prosperity out of one side of their mouth when they're in a church service or around an atmosphere that carries the anointing. On the other hand, their everyday life is consumed with talk about how hard it is, how high taxes are, how nobody could afford a place like that, on and on. Their poverty mindset destroys all of their actions that would otherwise lead to prosperity.

When Adalis and I were first married, I was preaching at a church and the pastor and his wife asked us to go to the mall one afternoon. While we were walking around, we came across a store that I'd never been to, which sold extremely expensive clothing. The pastor's wife said, "That's a very nice store, we can't shop in there. No Christians can shop in there." I was extremely bothered when she said that. I was poor with roughly $200 to my name. Nonetheless, just hearing someone say that ticked me off. I made up my mind right then and there that I was going to buy something, even if it was only a writing pen. So I said, "Adalis, let's go in there." We went in and I told her, "See if there are any shoes that you like." She saw a pair of boots that cost almost $1,200. I had nowhere near enough money to purchase them. As we were looking at the boots, the sales associate informed us that they'd been marked down. As it turned out, the boots were only $210. I put it on a credit card and we took them home. Adalis still has those boots, even after all these years. As I walked out of the store, the pastor's wife's jaw dropped. She said, "Oh, you bought something. How much did that cost?"

You see, I simply made up my mind that I am not going to be poor. Even back when I was poor, I determined that it was going to be a temporary situation. I would declare, "I'm coming out of this. I won't be poor." I refused to speak how other broke people spoke.

"We can't eat there."

"We can't shop there."

It's a necessity to have a picture in your spirit that you're a child of the Most High God and that the Word of God is true. If God calls you blessed, you are blessed. Quit speaking against the blessings. You can't say, "I will never have that. I don't know how anyone can afford that kind of thing."

Not long ago, I was out to eat with some faith preachers in the charismatic movement. They believe in prosperity and have Kenneth Copeland's books. Yet, all they talked about the whole meal was that they couldn't understand how anyone would spend money on a business class airplane ticket. Debating amongst themselves that a person's money could go to a better cause.

One important key to understand is that God doesn't need you to save money on one thing, so you can spend it on something else. There's enough money for you to buy a business class ticket to fly overseas, stay at a nice hotel, eat good food, feed the poor, and clothe the naked. You don't have to take money from one thing so you can have it for another thing. God is El Shaddai, the God of more than enough. He has enough for *all* those things.

Break the mentality of "How can you spend money on that, when you can spend money on this instead?" There is enough money for both things. It's not as though God only has enough money for you to either buy a business class ticket or pay your mortgage that month. God isn't like that, He has enough for everything. The problem isn't getting the money. The problem is with people's mindsets. For example, for generations some people have been conditioned by their parents and grandparents, to believe that cars and insurance are too expensive. Instead, they take the bus. It becomes a family cycle. To break that cycle, someone has to be the first to comprehend that the same faith you use for bus money can be used to purchase an automobile.

It's your mind that thinks small. And it will continue to do so, until you allow the Word of God to transform your mind. Paul admonished, let your mind be renewed by the washing of the water of the Word of God (Ephesians 5:26). Align your mind with the Word of God.

How Do You Break a Poverty Mentality?

In order to break a poverty mentality, you must think about money the way God thinks about money. You can't think about money the way Bernie Sanders thinks about money. You can't think about money the way Americans think about money. You can't think about money the way traditional churches think about money. Align your mind with the way God thinks.

God does not redistribute wealth from those with the most and spread it to those with the least. Throughout the Bible you'll find that God rewards production and punishes laziness and unfruitfulness. John 15:2 says, **"He cuts off every branch of mine that doesn't produce fruit, and he prunes the branches that do bear fruit so they will produce even more."**

If your mentality on money is shaped by public schools in America, you're never going to prosper. People in America have been trained to resent wealthy people. Refer to the passage in Luke 19:12-26. Jesus took from the man that only had one talent and gave it to the one that had ten. He took from the one that had the least and gave it to the one that had the most. The disciples objected to Jesus' reasoning. What did they think Jesus was going to say? "Oh, sorry I wasn't thinking. I meant to take five from the man that had ten and give them to the man that did poorly." No! Jesus said, **"...to those who use well what they are given, even more will be given. But from those who do nothing, even what little they have will be taken away"** (Luke 19:26).

Think of it like this, take everyone's money right now, put it in a big pot, and then distribute it evenly. Everyone gets a check for the same amount. Let's say everyone gets $400,000. Do you realize there would be people that would lose the entire $400,000 within 24 hours? They would go to a casino and lose all their money within 24 hours, ending up just as broke as they were prior. On the opposite side, there would be other people who would have millions of dollars within 30 days. Within another 90 days, they would be in the billions. Purely by doing the same thing they did with the initial $400,000. You can never spread everything evenly! That's not how things work.

You can be temporarily poor because of something that happened. You lose everything in a fire or you're laid off. However, if you're poor for long periods of time, it's because you don't manage money properly. Most of us who grew up in homes where our parents were in debt and struggling, have been passed down the same mentality.

"Life is hard."

"There's not enough money to do things."

"I don't know where rich people get their money?"

"I'll never have money like that."

They start speaking those words and their minds aren't lined up with the Word of God. We all love our parents, but if those of you who had poor parents were being honest, many of them weren't tithers. Many of them were content to work the same job. They weren't starting a company on the side and being diligent in business. It's not that life is too hard. Everyone, particularly in America, has the opportunity to do well, especially a Christian. God has promised to bless all the work that you carry out. Drop the excuses that life is too hard and that it's never worked out for your family. Make up your mind to start thinking about money the way God thinks about money. Instead of seeing someone with money and automatically crinkling your nose, take some notes on what they're doing that's different. It could be your ticket to a place of abundance.

Some people may question why would a person need all this money? As someone that gave away close to $1 million last year – I can say that it's very nice to be able to call a church in India, ask how much money they need to finish building their church, and simply send the amount to their banking account. It's incredible to be able to call a church in Congo and send them money to finish their roof. The abundance God entrusts you with enables you to be the answer to other people's prayers. God wants you to be a financial solution to the problems in this world. To get there, you have to break a poverty mentality.

See God as Your Sole Financial Source

In Genesis 17, God appeared to Abraham and said "I am El Shaddai – the God of more than enough." In this passage, God was revealing himself to Abraham as the all-sufficient Provider. He was telling Abraham that, even though he was going to live in a foreign land with the Philistines, he would never need their help for anything. He was essentially telling Abraham, "Look to me only, and I will provide everything."

If you see God as your sole financial provider, you never look to man for anything. You look to God for everything. You have two eyes in your head: can you make one eye look up at the sky while the other eye is looking down at the ground at the same time? Try it and you'll discover that it's impossible. You can either look up or look down. In the same way, you can't look to both God and people for your financial solutions.

Ever since God has blessed our ministry, people ask us all the time for money to help them pay their bills. They would rather have me give them money than discover the principles of God's Word that I learned, which put me in the position to give money. Most people would rather know someone that has money than know what God's Word says, hide it in their heart, and produce the money themselves.

Bishop Oyedepo tells a story about a time when he was still poor in the ministry. The man he worked under had a worldwide ministry and had just come back from speaking in America. He had a duffel bag full of cash from all the offerings he had received. He loved Bishop Oyedepo and told him he could take as much money as he wanted from the bag. Bishop Oyedepo said, "Sir, I don't want the money that's in the bag. I want what you know that caused there to be money in the bag."

The majority of people are not interested in doing things that way. If you're going to be blessed, you need to make today the last day that you ever ask anyone for anything. Don't ask people for rides. Don't ask people for food. If you're going to be the lender and not the borrower, quit borrowing. Be the person that provides rides and gives to the poor. You can't go to a place of abundance with a needy mentality.

Some people are always asking for something: "I don't have money to go out to eat. Can you pay for me this time? Can you give me a ride to church? I don't have a car." Learn to access God's power to provide for your needs, or you will never get to a place of abundance. I won't ever need to be concerned with not having anything, because I know God will keep His promise. God keeps His covenant. But just for the sake of this point, I would rather die on a bus stop bench with my dignity, than ask people for help with my bills. If you're in debt or constantly running short at the end of the month, you don't need people to give you money to help with your bills. You need to figure out what you're doing wrong that's causing more money to go out, than come in each month. Sort things out yourself and learn to look to God for your financial help.

Our ministry didn't get to where it is by asking people for money. There's a man on our Board of Directors who is the president of a bank. He has a multimillion-dollar salary. I've never called him and said, "We have crusades coming up. They are going to cost roughly $100,000 each. I just wanted to ask you to pray about what you would give." I don't operate that way. I've never contacted anyone privately to ask for financial help. In the early days, when I found myself in a bind, my wife and I would pray. We'd ask the Lord, "Father, show us what we're doing wrong. Bail us out. We know this is our fault. But we lean on your mercy to help us out of this jam." And God would help us. That's where miracles come from! They don't come from looking to people, like your rich uncle or father.

People always want a hand out. I've learned that people never just give something without wanting something in return. When I give, I don't keep track of what I'm giving. I know someone who always brings up the fact that he gave $1,000 to a ministry and never even received a thank you letter. Who cares? Would he be more satisfied, all these years later, if he was holding a thank you card in his hands? Why are you giving? You should be giving to the Lord regardless of what the person or ministry thinks of it. You give directed by the Spirit as unto the Lord. The little trinket from their ministry or thank you letter shouldn't be the motivation of your giving.

I will only lean on God for my provision. If you can't afford to go out to eat, don't go out to eat. If you can't afford things that you've made a part of your monthly bills, cut them out. You can live without cable. You can live without Internet. Until you get your finances in order, stop running your budget where you find yourself in a deficit and have to ask people for help. You will never get ahead. That's how poor people operate. You can't act like a beggar if you're going to come into abundance.

God Has Decreed Your Ability to Rise to the Top

Where God is taking you doesn't have to involve debt. Our ministry is not debt-free. Our ministry has never had any debt to be free from. We pay cash for everything. I never had credit, which is one of the reasons I learned to operate this way. I didn't even have good enough credit to fall into debt.

Our ministry doesn't "launch out in faith" and then believe for the money to come in. I have a budget. I know what's projected to come in each month and we pay far less than that amount in bills and expenses. I don't buy a house "by faith." I don't buy a car "by faith." I have a budgeted amount that takes no prayer and no believing God whatsoever. It's planned out. Don't use faith for purchases, make a plan.

Make a Plan

God wants planning. There's power in wise planning. The Bible speaks about it a host of times in Proverbs. People will say, "You're going to college, you need student loans. You're launching a business, you need a commercial loan to buy your property." Deuteronomy 15:6 says, **"For the LORD your God will bless you as He has promised you, you will lend money to many nations but will never need to borrow..."**

Everything our ministry owns has been paid for in full. When we bought the SUV for our ministry, I wrote one check for it at the dealership. You don't have to live in debt. Debt is not a sin, but debt is a weight. You end up paying 30-70% more than what something is worth, because you either didn't have the faith for the money ahead of time or are buying something that's beyond your price range. Buy what you can afford. Ride a 12-speed bike with pride that you purchased with cash before you go into debt. It's funny how the owner of a two-door Chevrolet can look at someone driving a BMW and chide, "How could they spend all that money on that car?!" When in reality, if the

BMW was purchased with cash and the Chevy was financed for 6 years, the Chevy will end up costing more than the BMW. Debt is an enslaving thing.

When you go into debt you're telling God, "I'm much bigger than you think I am. Let me prove it to you." The money you have right now is an indication of how fruitful you are. Don't buy things that are for someone 10x more fruitful. Until you hit that level of fruitfulness, you're going to kill yourself trying to have those things.

When I was 19 years old, I used to view people in church that had a luxury car and big house and think, "Man, they are rich!" Then you start spending time with them and realize in reality, they are not rich. They're in debt up to their eyeballs and can't sleep at night, trying to make it appear like they're prosperous. God didn't make His covenant in the Bible so that you can *appear* to be rich. The blessing of God *actually* makes you rich. Stop trying to appear to be something you are not! Be content to be where you are, while at the same time, believing to move forward.

Don't be a fool who wears a $2,500 watch and an outfit that costs 10x more than the amount of money you have in the bank. You look rich but you're broke. You're just a poor person wearing expensive clothes. *Be* prosperous, don't just *look* prosperous. God gave you the ability to be prosperous and you don't need debt to accomplish it. Allow these words to free you from the ensnarement of debt: *If God can't take me there, may I never go. If God can't give it to me, may I never have it. If God can't do it, let it remain undone.*

Stop striving beyond where God is taking you. God will promise you an Isaac like he did for Abraham, but along the way you'll have the opportunity to give birth to an Ishmael. When you don't see the promise manifest, you can make a plan in the flesh to have what God said you can have, but it will always end with problems. Be patient in faith, knowing that your beginnings – though they may be small – will later speak. The Bible says wait for the vision, though it tarries, for it shall speak at the end (Habakkuk 2:3). Do not despise the day of small beginnings, for your latter end will be greater than the former (Job 8:7). Don't rush.

I would love to be on primetime ABC television five nights a week, but I'm not there yet. I will get there, but I won't put myself in debt trying to make something happen. There will come a day when it will be easy for me to fill that television spot, and then I'll do it. God has decreed your ability to rise to the top without debt. Get out of an indebted lifestyle. Live within your means or better yet, live below your means. You'll escape pressure.

Furthermore, when you're in debt, you're making other people rich. Do you know why the banks have such beautiful downtown skyscrapers? They entice prospective home owners to purchase a $280,000 house on a 30-year note. Then by the time they've finished paying off the loan, they've actually paid $700,000. You've got to break that cycle and allow God to show you a way to get to the top without debt.

Expect the Desires of Your Heart to Be Met

"Take delight in the LORD, and he will give you your heart's desires."

PSALMS 37:4

God will give you the desires of your heart. A poverty mentality believes for your needs to be met. You should have faith that God is going to anoint your head with oil and your cup of blessing will overflow. He'll not only meet your needs, He'll fill your storehouses with grain.

A poverty mentality has you pray for food and clothes for today and pajamas to wear for tonight. Think beyond that mentality. Begin to thank God that He's not only going to meet your needs; He's going to give you an overflow so you can meet the needs of your hurting world. He's going to give you the desires of your heart as you put His kingdom first. He didn't say, "Seek ye first the kingdom of God and his righteousness, and He'll meet your needs." He said, "Seek ye first the kingdom of God and his righteousness and all the other things that you could be out there busting your rear end trying to get, I will add them unto you" (My own interpretation of Matthew 6:33).

Let me tell you a story. My father loves to hunt. He isn't the type that would spend money on a large hunting expedition. There was a man who got saved at one of his crusades and was later going on a $30,000 dollar hunting expedition to the Hebrides Islands in Scotland. It was a nonrefundable trip. One of the other men who had signed up for the trip had an unexpected death in his family, and

15

was now unable to attend. The man who was saved at the crusade called my father up and said, "If you can get a flight to Scotland, you can have this $30,000 dollar hunt for the price of an airline ticket." My dad traveled to Scotland and stayed in a five-star lodge, hunted blackface ram in the Hebrides Islands, and shot a world record blackface ram on that hunt. That can only be attributed to the Lord.

God didn't do that for me, I hate the outdoors. God did that for my father. He knows my dad loves to hunt, so He gave him a world-class hunting trip for a small percentage of the actual price. God knows what you like! He won't just meet your needs; He'll bless you when you keep His kingdom first. Believe that way! Take your eyes off your daily needs and start thanking God that He's going to give you the desires of your heart.

Make today the last day that you ever say, "That's expensive." That's how poor people talk. You won't hear Bill Gates say something's expensive. Expensive is a word poor people use in their vocabulary. Where is that in the Bible? John 6 chronicles the feeding of the 5,000 that contrasts man's poverty mindset with God's abundant mindset. The disciples told Jesus, "Listen, these people have been following us for 3 days and haven't eaten. If we don't send them away, they are going to want food, and *we* are going to be on the hook for it." Jesus said, "You feed them." The disciples were trying to get out of the bill. Jesus said, "We are going to take care of the bill."

The disciples responded and said, "Master, that will cost a small fortune. That's expensive." Jesus said, "Tell them to sit down in groups of 50 or 100 and that I will be with them shortly." Then Jesus took care of the problem. The disciples only thought about how expensive it was, but Jesus' mind didn't work that way. His mind made a plan using the supernatural power of the Holy Spirit to feed 5,000 men.

Notice Jesus didn't say, "I don't know how we're going to do that, that's so expensive." Jesus fixed his mind on the abundance of God and made a plan to feed the multitude. If you're going to have the Jesus-type of abundance, you need to have the mind of Christ. Christ's mind wasn't one that thought, "It will cost a small fortune to feed this many people." Jesus never let those words come out of His mouth. If Jesus refused to say it was expensive to feed 5,000 men (plus the women and children) then you have no business calling a shirt expensive, a car expensive, or flying in first class expensive. It's not expensive. You have a small mind – that's the problem. Nothing is expensive. Your Father owns all the silver and all the gold (Haggai 2:8).

Never Say, "I Can't Afford That"

Instead say, "I will be back for you later." Stop saying, "I can't sit in first class, I can't eat in that restaurant, I can't wear those kinds of clothes." For surely, you never will. I'm not advocating developing a mentality where you're aiming for clothes and first class flights. Simply be open to God blessing you and making a way to purchase those things, as easy as it is to buy a 3-pack of t-shirts. There will come a day when you'll shop in any store you want and not have to look at the price tags. It will be such a small percentage of your income as you engage these other principles. The Bible says he who gives to the poor will never lack anything. God has promised that as you engage His covenant, you won't need to worry about the price of gasoline. Jesus said why concern yourself with these things? As we read earlier, this is how the heathen think. Your Father will take good care of you (Matthew 6:32).

Wherever you are right now, I want you to say these things out loud: *My Father will take good care of me. He knows what I like to wear. He knows what I like to eat. He's not going to have me scrape by. He's going to take good care of me.*

As you train your mind and words to be likewise, don't join in certain conversations. Where people are sitting around saying, "It's expensive to stay at a place like that. I don't know how they can take 10 days of vacation? That's awfully expensive." Don't join in and say, "Yeah, I don't know how either." At least remain quiet and be neutral. It would be better, however, to go to the opposite extreme and say, "I'm going to take 14 days of vacation."

Let broke people think broke thoughts and say broke things. Don't join in with them. Think abundant thoughts and say abundant things. It will make your spouse happy. Even if you can't afford to eat there today, drive by Ruth's Chris Steak House and say, "One day soon, you and I will be eating there."

I heard Pastor Enoch Adeboye share a similar story that almost brought me to tears. When he and his wife were young, they were so poor that they were splitting a nut for dinner. They got a nut from a tree, boiled it, cut it in half and ate it together. While they were eating, something arose in his spirit. He looked at his wife across the table and said, "You know, we won't always be eating like this." Then he started to describe what they would have on the table as their first course, their second course, and so on. The Bible says, **"A man's belly shall be satisfied with the fruit of his mouth; and with the harvest of his lips shall he be filled"** (Proverbs 18:20, KJV). God hears what you say. When you begin to speak that way, God will see those words come to pass in your life.

Never Say, "I Can't Wear That"

"Evil people may have piles of money and may store away mounds of clothing. But the righteous will wear that clothing, and the innocent will divide that money."

JOB 27:16-17

In over 18 years of Sunday school and youth group, I don't recall ever having Job 27:16-17 as a memory verse. The Bible says that you will wear and spend what the wicked people are flaunting. Don't say that you can't wear those kinds of clothes. It's not something that you'll have to strive for. Make establishing the kingdom of God the thing you strive for, and God will add those other things unto you. One time the Lord spoke to my spirit to stop spending money on clothes and instead, give that money to a woman I knew. This woman was going to open up a restaurant and feed the homeless for free. For a year and a half, I didn't buy any clothes. Any time I felt like buying clothes, I would give that amount of money to missions.

Sometime later, my wife and I were shopping at the outlets. While Adalis was shopping, I was sitting in the car listening to sports radio. I felt the Lord speak to me to go into the Burberry outlet. I went in and there was only one suit in my size. It was price tagged at $1,400 dollars. I didn't have nearly enough money, but I felt the Lord tell me to purchase it. I brought it to the sales register and thought that I'd at least look like I was being obedient to God. When they rang up the $1,400 suit, it registered at $112. The cashier was in disbelief and scanned it again. She continued to rescan it, becoming more frustrated each time. Finally she called the manager who said, "If that's what it rings up as then that's what you have to sell it for." The suit cost more to make than what I paid. I bought my first luxury suit for $112. The blessings didn't stop after that.

As I was obedient to God and continued to sow that clothing money, the blessings continued. There was a pastor I preached for in Virginia who took me out to eat in Washington, D.C. When I met him at the restaurant, he told me to follow him as he proceeded to a suit store down the street. He said, "Do you like any of these suits?" I replied, "Yes." He said, "Do you like all of them?" I replied, "Yes." He took the three suits off the rack, put his credit card down, and bought me three suits that were $1,200 apiece. That's $3,600 in total worth of suits. He handed them to me and said, "You'll wear these suits and preach the gospel all over the world." And I have done just that.

There's a man who works at an Ellie Tahari Warehouse and gives me two or three suits every time I go to Montreal, Canada. The only time I buy clothes is when I don't pack enough or a meeting gets extended. People give me incredibly nice clothes, left and right. Even when I didn't have money, I never let the following come out of my mouth, "I don't know how any preacher can wear suits like that. I could never spend that much money on a suit." No – I was open to it. "Lord if you want to bless me, I'm here to be blessed." I don't believe that some adulterous, cigar-smoking businessman can wear a Versace suit, and I can't.

A person doesn't look poor because they have poor clothing. They look poor because they don't value their clothing. I came across an article in a magazine that showed two men wearing suits. One was wearing a $5,000 suit and the other a $300 suit. The man wearing the $5,000 suit didn't have it tailored or pressed. The man in the $300 tailored and pressed suit looked sharper. The article described that you always look better in a cheaper suit that is well cared for. Let me reiterate, you don't look poor because your clothes don't have value. You look poor because you don't value your clothes. Look sharp and dress well. When you go out, you are representing the kingdom of God. Dress like someone that makes people want to know what God you serve. If you're going through a hard time, you don't have to reflect it in your appearance. If you just lost your job, don't put on a hooded sweatshirt and dirty jeans while walking around with poor posture. Carry yourself like a child of God and be open to wearing the best.

"And why worry about your clothing? Look at the lilies of the field and how they grow. They don't work or make their clothing, yet Solomon in all his glory was not dressed as beautifully as they are."

MATTHEW 6:28-29

How much more would your Father, not give you sharp, nice clothing? God owns all the silver and all the gold. He owns everything. I love to see my daughter wearing the best clothes. She's my daughter and I want to give her the best that I can. That's how God feels about you. Don't cut off what He can do by letting stupid things come out of your mouth like, "I would never spend that on a suit." After all, who says *you* are going to have to spend it? The same way God provided, without me having to ask anyone, God will provide for you.

Never Say, "We Can't Eat There"

This principle also refers back to Job 27:16-17. Don't look at restaurants and say you can't go in because it's too expensive. Quit talking like that. You can eat there. At least have enough faith to look at the menu and you might find out that it's not as expensive as you thought.

You can eat the best. You don't have to eat garbage and end up with diabetes. Your pancreas and kidneys don't have to shut down because you're always looking for the cheapest, processed, fried food. You can eat what you like. You don't have to pick between feeding the poor and feeding yourself. God has enough money to do both.

Have a Financial Plan

A poverty mindset never has a financial plan. You should know how much money is coming in and how much is going out. Factor in tithes, offerings, and savings. The Bible says a fool spends everything he gets (Proverbs 21:20).

You must have a source of income. "I'm trusting God" is not a source of income. Abraham trusted God, and he worked as a cattle rancher. God will bless the work of your hands. If you don't work, you will never be blessed. There needs to be something your hands are doing that makes money.

Look For Who to Bless, Not For Who Will Bless You

Every church I go to I think, "Who's going to be there? Is there anyone that's in the ministry that I can sow into? Is there a need the church has? Are they replacing a roof? Are they building an addition? Is there something that I can do to help them and be a blessing?" I don't go there wondering about what the people are going to do for me. I don't send a list of demands and say I need $3,500 a night. I come with money in my pocket. I look for people to bless.

You can shock people, even by the smallest gestures. I preached for an 81 year old pastor and took him and his wife out to eat. They ordered a soup and salad, just one of each between the two. I gave the waiter my card ahead of time and paid for the meal. The pastor said, "Oh, you didn't have to do that. I can't believe you paid for our meal." I said, "Don't worry about it, the bill came to $18." He replied, "No, it's not about the cost of the bill. I've been a pastor for 60 years and you're the first evangelist that's ever paid for a meal."

Why is it that so many evangelists never pay for anything? They save all their receipts and submit them at the end of the week to get reimbursed. Reimbursed for travel, plane tickets, rental cars, and food. I refuse to believe that way. Train yourself to look for someone to bless, not how to get others to bless you. If you give you'll never have to worry about receiving, *ever*.

In Genesis 18 Abraham noticed men standing outside that he hadn't come across prior. He ran out and asked them if they had anything to eat. When he found out they hadn't, he told them not to leave until his wife cooked them food and they refreshed themselves with water (Genesis 18:4-5).

The Bible says if you're the seed of Abraham, you will do the works that Abraham did (John 8:39). Abraham was a giver. Imagine the mentality to see strangers out in the field and question if they've had anything to eat. If you want to have Abraham's blessing, you have to do the works Abraham did. Look for people to bless.

Be Thankful

Thankfulness causes everything to multiply. Before Jesus multiplied the food, he gave thanks for the young boy's lunch (John 6:11). It wasn't until after he gave thanks that it was multiplied. Before Jesus raised Lazarus from the dead, he thanked God.

Before anything multiplies, you have to be thankful. A poverty mindset is one of unthankfulness. Poor people focus on who wronged them, who should've done more for them, who broke a promise, etc. Poor people can always identify who was supposed to pay them and didn't, who was supposed to help them and didn't, who they've helped and never received anything from in return. They are always complaining.

Be thankful you're alive. Thank God that you have lungs that breathe air. Thank God that you have a sharp mind and are anointed to produce wealth. Be thankful God's hand is on your life. Be thankful that you have the Word of God and God's covenant in effect today. Be thankful that the money in your pocket right now will never finish. Be thankful that today is the poorest that you will ever be. That from this day forward, goodness and mercy will follow you every day of your life, and the blessings of God will pursue and overtake everything you do.

There's so much in life to be thankful for. Who cares who should've done more for you and didn't. God is your source, not people. As long as you stay thankful, God will continue to multiply, just as He did with the little boy's lunch (John 6). As you give thanks, what isn't enough will turn into *more* than enough, to feed a multitude with baskets left over.

Chapter 2

Breaking Materialism

"Do not love this world nor the things it offers you, for when you love the world, you do not have the love of the Father in you. For the world offers only a craving for physical pleasure, a craving for everything we see, and pride in our achievements and possessions. These are not from the Father, but are from this world. And this world is fading away, along with everything that people crave. But anyone who does what pleases God will live."

1 JOHN 2:15-17

The Bible says there's a contrast between loving God and loving the world. When Jesus spoke regarding *love of the world*, He was referring to things that are in the world. You can't have God bless you and take you to His riches, if you're carrying a love for material possessions.

You may not realize it, but you most likely deal with materialism. I didn't realize it when I dealt with materialism. If God blessed you right now with $1 million dollars, you would spend it on worldly things that you enjoy. I don't believe that God will take you to the place He desires for your life, until materialism is broken.

Let's break down my definition of *breaking materialism*. It's not along the lines of your common church sermon, where I profess to not caring about anything and drive a car held together by Christian bumper stickers. Dr. Rodney Howard-Browne shared a story of the time the Lord spoke to him saying, "When everything means nothing to you, I will give you everything." Let that statement resonate in your spirit.

When everything means nothing to you,
I will give you everything.

In the last chapter, I shared the story of when the Lord told me to take all the money I was spending on clothes and give it to missions. When I stopped spending money on clothes, I realized just how much I'd been spending. I was single and wanted to look presentable in case the Lord brought a woman into my life to marry. I didn't want to look like an unkempt slob. As an evangelist, you're always in front of a new crowd, who are judging you based solely on your appearance. There's nothing wrong with wanting to look sharp.

After a year and a half of not spending money on clothes, materialism became erased from my system. In essence, the Lord stopped me from buying cheap suits during that time. When I did, He gave me the nicest suits I ever owned. All kinds of clothes have been coming in ever since. It all started with God breaking materialism off my life.

If the Lord had given us $1 million dollars five years ago, it would have been spent much differently. I'd like to say we wouldn't have spent it on ourselves. Nor taken a housing allowance and paid cash for an extremely nice house. Receiving that amount now, however, gave us the ability to give employees in our ministry a raise and the ability to give $400,000 outside the ministry.

"Seek the Kingdom of God above all else, and live righteously, and he will give you everything you need."

MATTHEW 6:33

You don't have to make a decision to never have anything nice. When God told me to quit buying clothes, it didn't mean I would never have new clothes. It was actually the opposite. I now have both finer and vastly more clothes than I did when I was shopping all the time. Before that, anytime someone gave me money, I was off to the mall to buy something for myself. Now there's no need to go because the blessing chases me. God changed my heart and the kingdom of God became my number one priority.

Make it your business to establish the kingdom of God. When you do, God will add unto you, all the other things that you were pursuing. You won't have to remind Him. You won't have to pray about it. God will make sure that they chase you down.

When I was spending all my money on myself, I never had people say, "I feel like I need to do something for you, come and meet me at my suit store," or "I want to give you something so you can go on vacation." I was too busy spending money on those things for myself. However, when I took that money and used it for God's kingdom instead, He put people in place to grant me the desires of my heart. *When everything means nothing to you, God will give you everything.*

"Labour not to be rich: cease from thine own wisdom" (Proverbs 23:4, KJV). Anti-prosperity people often like to reference this verse. Yet, they fail to interpret it correctly. You're not laboring to be rich. My ministry does a tremendous amount of work, but our goal isn't to find a way to personally enrich ourselves under the guise of doing ministry. Our hearts are set on establishing the kingdom of God. That's our heartbeat. God promised He would bless us if we put Him first. **"The blessing of the Lord makes a person rich, and he adds no sorrow with it"** (Proverbs 10:22). It doesn't say His blessing "meets a man's needs," it says it, "makes a person rich."

A while back, I was sitting on a first class flight next to a woman drinking an alcoholic beverage. Many people become talkative when they drink and this woman was not the exception. She talked incessantly the whole flight. Two hours into the flight she asked, "So what is it that you do for a living?" I didn't care to tell her. When you tell people you're a preacher, you usually have to listen to their thoughts on preachers and Christianity. She kept pressing, so I eventually told her. She was surprised I was sitting in first class and said, "I thought you guys were supposed to give all your money away to the poor." I replied, "I've been trying to give all my money away to the poor, but the more I give, the more it keeps pouring back."

You don't have to choose. Saying, "Instead of me having nice things, I'm going to take the money I would spend on myself and give it to the kingdom of God for souls." Or, "We've never had anything nice because everything we have, we've given to the ministry." We've all heard or known someone who's said those things. I don't believe them. Jesus said, **"Give, and you [not other people] will receive. Your gift will return to you in full – pressed down, shaken together to make room for more, running over and poured into your lap"** (Luke 6:38; emphasis and brackets added). It's impossible to give your money and sacrifice to establish God's kingdom, and be left with nothing in the end. Jesus said in Acts 20:35, **"...It is more blessed to give than to receive."** The blessing stays with me.

"Then these righteous ones will reply, 'Lord, when did we ever see you hungry and feed you? Or thirsty and give you something to drink? Or a stranger and show you hospitality? Or naked and give you clothing? When did we ever see you sick or in prison and visit you?' And the King will say, 'I tell you the truth, when you did it to one of the least of these my brothers and sisters, you were doing it to me!'"

MATTHEW 25:37-40

There are three ways you can allow the grace that breaks materialism to flow in your life: immerse yourself in human need, immerse yourself in the cause of reaching the lost, and give.

Immerse Yourself in Human Need

T.L. Osborn said that every Christian should immerse themselves in human need. What does that statement mean? If you look at who I follow on Twitter, you'll find that I follow news agencies that cover what's going on with

31

Christians in Syria, the Middle East, Pakistan, and Southeast Asia. I force myself to look at the pictures of a four year old boy holding his two year old sister because both of their parents died in an earthquake. I make myself look at pictures of massacred Christians in Pakistan. I refuse to look at the blurred or blacked out photos. I look at the ones of people crying, lying on the ground with part of their leg blown off. When you see those images, it's difficult to be a Christian that gives a testimony about the difficult year you've had because you were expecting a promotion at your job – "I didn't get the promotion. We promised our kids that we'd put in a swimming pool and now we're unable."

Stop living your life where you become distraught over every little thing that happens. Immerse yourself in actual human need – people who are dying, people who don't have food, people who need help. Make it your business. You can't look at it and not want to do something.

On the other hand, if you immerse yourself in the materialistic celebrity culture, you're going to become materialistic. You'll only care about things that don't matter. Proverbs 4:23 says, **"Guard your heart above all else, for it determines the course of your life."** If what you look at controls the desires of your heart, then don't look at luxury magazines. It will create a desire for those material goods. You can't break materialism if you're surrounding yourself with things that feed materialism. Break materialism by immersing yourself in human need.

On social media, I follow accounts that show the plight of the persecuted church. Materialism can never grow in my heart because the thing I'm most immersed in is human need. I don't let too many days pass by where I'm not looking at their starving faces. That desire did not come by accident, it was cultivated.

Make an effort to know what's going on with your Christian brothers and sisters in Pakistan, North Africa, Sudan, Southeast Asia, and Myanmar. Don't settle to hear about it every once in awhile. Make it a point to do your research. If you don't know then you don't care. Don't be someone that has no clue about what's happening in the world, simply because it's not happening in America. Care about your Christian brothers and sisters *all over the world*. When you see what they go through, it will birth a desire to help.

Immerse Yourself in the Cause of Reaching the Lost

If you're in the business field, make it your goal to have the bulk of your revenue go to establishing the kingdom of God. Prior to receiving a million dollar offering our largest ministry expense was, and still is, giving. It makes it a very delightful organization to run. When you make giving your highest priority, then money begins to flow like tap water. Our giving is greater than what we pay for salaries or television air time.

Find people that are winning souls. We support ministries outside our own. John Osteen, Joel Osteen's father, used to spend his entire Monday signing checks to send to missionaries. There's a secret in getting to the top – care about what's going on in the world. Not only to give hurting people food, blankets, and clothing but to ensure the salvation of their souls.

Don't leave the work to people who are essentially tourists overseas for four years under the guise of missions work, because they don't get anyone saved. Some people only have PowerPoint slides of people they met and stories about how hard it is to live in a third world country. Find people who are winning the lost and become immersed in their ministries. Look at the pictures of what they are doing. Let it move your heart. If it moves your heart, it will move your money.

Give

Allow the giving grace to come upon your life. God established giving as a foolproof plan to never allow materialism to hold you captive. When you choose to sit back in your seat and do nothing, you're in essence showing God, "I'm completely unmoved by your kingdom. You're not going to get $1 dollar from me." Then God knows that this world has a hold on your heart.

God hates greed. You can't be a giver and greedy, they're contradictory terms. Greedy people don't give and givers lack greed. Some Christians say, "If God blesses you then money will take the place of God in your heart." No, it won't. The Bible says in Deuteronomy 8:12-13, **"For when you have become full and prosperous and have built fine homes to live in, and when your flocks and herds have become very large and your silver and gold have multiplied along with everything else, be careful!"**

When 1 million dollars came into our possession I said, "We need to be careful now. We have a lot of money." I know two other ministries that were given 1 million dollars within the last ten years, and are now in worse financial shape than they've ever been. As soon as the money came in they went into protection mode. They didn't tithe off the million and the curse came. I made sure to say, "God not only are we going to give 10% we're going to give an additional 30% to let you know that the more you bless us, the less money has a hold on our hearts. The more you bless us, the more we are going to give."

Let's look at Paul's words in 2 Corinthians 8:1-8, **"Now I want you to know, dear brothers and sisters, what God in his kindness has done through the churches in Macedonia. They are being tested by many troubles, and they are very poor. But they are also filled with abundant joy, which has overflowed in rich generosity. For I can testify that they gave not only what they could afford, but far more. And they did it of their own free will. They begged us again and again for the privilege of sharing in the gift for the believers in Jerusalem. They even did more than we had hoped, for their first action was to give themselves to the Lord and to us, just as God wanted them to do. So we have urged Titus, who encouraged your giving in the first place, to return to you and encourage you to finish this ministry of giving. Since you excel in so many ways – in your faith, your gifted speakers, your knowledge, your enthusiasm, and your love from us – I want you to excel also in this gracious act of giving. I am not commanding you to do**

this. But I am testing how genuine your love is by comparing it with the eagerness of the other churches."

Giving proves your love to God. To give far more than you can afford is a supernatural thing. The devil steals, man hoards, and God gives. It's a person's nature to keep everything they have. Allow God to break that off your life. I've watched the way my 4 year old daughter plays with smaller children. There will be nine toys and she'll take all nine toys and walk away. The other child will follow her asking, "Can I have one?" When I tell her to share the toys she immediately starts to cry, when they weren't even her toys to begin with!

People want to hoard everything. Don't allow yourself to fall into that category. Enter into the giving grace today and allow yourself to become a big giver. I emptied out my bank account two times before I was 25 years old. It seemed like such a big thing at the time. The amounts I gave are very small to me now, because I've proved to God that anything He gives me, I'll give back at any time. Abraham placing Isaac on the altar is a grace from God. God sending his only begotten Son is the nature of God. God desires us to have that same nature. If God wouldn't spare His own Son, how can you hold back any material possession?

Allow the giving grace to become a part of your life. Every time you give your tithe, it's proof to God that money has no hold on your life. Your offering is proof to God that your love for Him and His kingdom is real. Your offering says, "God I have a right to spend this on anything I want, but what I want is to give it into your hands." Then

God automatically knows you have no greed and no love for this world. You qualify as someone that God can bless.

Pray this prayer: *I pray that every trace of American materialism or Western greed that's anywhere lurking in my spirit will be destroyed right now, in Jesus' name. By that same grace of the Holy Spirit, there will be a desire in my heart to give. When I'm in a restaurant and see another table of people from church, I won't only pay for my own meal, I'll pay for theirs too. May I have eyes like Abraham and Jesus, to look for who to bless, not for who will bless me. And as I do so, all the things that other people are striving to attain, will be added unto me. In Jesus' name, Amen.*

Chapter 3

Breaking Company with Stagnant People

"He who walks with wise men will be wise, but the companion of fools will be destroyed."

PROVERBS 13:20, NKJV

Most people receive advice from other people's failures. They don't get married because their mother, who could never remain married, told them how awful marriage is. Their father who walked out tells them not to trust women. They listen to failures, and then they become a failure.

The people you choose to run with in life are the people you're going to become in life. You can't enter into wealth hanging around Christians who despise wealth and prosperity. I'm not saying you have to dump all your poor and middle-class friends and make rich friends, but be intentional with who you spend your time.

When the Bible talks about an equal yoke, it's not only talking about marrying someone that's a Christian. If you've been in church for any period of time, you've heard someone mention having an unequal yoke. This is a reference to 2 Corinthians 6:14 (NIV) which reads, **"Do not be yoked together with unbelievers. For what do righteousness and wickedness have in common? Or what fellowship can light have with darkness?"** This verse can be cross referenced to Deuteronomy 22:10, that says if two animals are plowing in a field together and they're not equally yoked, then one has to pull more weight. As you can see, being equally yoked does not only apply to marriage, but to everything you do in life – such as a business partner or a friend. You want to yoke or attach yourself to people that are headed in the same direction and believe the same thing. Amos 3:3 asks, **"Can two people walk together without agreeing on the direction?"** You can't move forward if you're knitted to people that enjoy moving backwards.

You have to find people that believe in what you do. Most people make the mistake of hanging out with whoever they end up with – "Hey, we grew up together. We went to fourth grade together." When you become an adult, none of that should matter anymore. You must learn to fundamentally abandon the people who refuse to progress. I'm not advocating that you should abandon people that need help. What I am saying is that most of us know a friend that is not blessed, and has no interest in being blessed. Furthermore, they don't care to hear about what you have to say on the subject. You can't waste your life hoping they'll come around. What you ought to do is pray for them, but leave it to the Lord. Let the Lord send someone new along their path.

Jesus said in Matthew 10:14, **"If any household or town refuses to welcome you or listen to your message, shake its dust from your feet as you leave."** He didn't say, "Ignore what the town says and go in regardless." He said if a city doesn't receive your message, shake the dust off your feet and condemn that city to its death. The same is true for people. You can waste your whole life trying to win someone to the Lord, who wants nothing whatsoever to do with the Lord. Meanwhile, in the time you've spent doing so, you could've led 250 other people to Jesus Christ.

"The Lord had said to Abram, 'Leave your native country, your relatives, and your father's family, and go to the land that I will show you. I will make you into a great nation. I will bless you and make you famous, and you will be a blessing to others. I will bless those who bless you and curse those who treat you with contempt. All the families on earth will be blessed through you.'"

GENESIS 12:1-3

Most people are accepting when you start to move forward in life. That is, until you start to pass their success. If you start to engage prosperity more than someone else, it's very common that you'll hear people say things like – "I think you're taking this a little too seriously. I think you're giving too much. You know tithing isn't in the New Testament."

Why surround yourself with people you have to fight with? I estimate that 90% of Christians try to walk with people with whom they have no agreement. They either don't believe in healing the way you do or they don't believe in prosperity. You don't build each other up when

41

you're together because you avoid subjects that might cause an argument. There's nothing wrong with ministering to people that disagree with you. However, when it comes to your close circle of friends, it's essential to choose people that are moving forward.

"...Imitate those who through faith and patience inherit what has been promised."

HEBREWS 6:12, NIV

Surround yourself with people who are going to the top, people that despise poverty, and value hard work. Surround yourself with people that don't see being rich as a bad thing. If you follow someone closely, you're going to pick up their impartation. Everything that's in that person's life will begin to flow into you. Don't merely become enamored by the fact that they're blessed, have nice suits, or seem to be a good speaker. Look at their life and fruit.

On one hand, someone may be doing well in some areas. You notice they're still with their first wife and have good children. On the other hand, they're anti-prosperity and their ministry is broke. They need to have a bake sale, fashion show, or chicken dinner if they want to do anything with the church. Their ministry always has a need and is struggling financially. I wouldn't go as far and say not to talk to someone like that, but I wouldn't model my life after someone that's struggling in any shape or form.

I've located people that run struggle-free ministries. For example, Kenneth Copeland has given 27 aircrafts to other ministries. Christians who believe like Kenneth Copeland and want something – purchase it. An illustration of this would be Bishop David Oyedepo, who never took an offering to purchase his plane. There's no pressure placed on the members of his church. At services they don't say, "I believe there are 7 people here that are going to sow $2,017 to represent the year 2017, and they'll lose God's favor if they refuse." Model yourself after people that are doing it right.

I was with a minister not long ago who is a part of a traditional denomination. He shared with me that he no longer attends district councils or sectional meetings for that denomination. He stated that he didn't want any of those ministers laying hands on him, because they don't believe in what he believes. He believes in healing and prosperity and they don't. Unfortunately, he's just as foolish as those men because he remains in that fellowship. Don't stay in men's company to be a big fish in a small pond – that's how people waste their lives. Ministers stay in denominations they don't agree with, don't receive anything from, and don't even attend their meetings. Why? Break away from them. Find people who believe what you believe, are headed in the direction you want to go, and join alongside them.

People who are not ministers do the same thing. They go to a dead church that doesn't believe in prosperity. If you desire to grow and believe God wants to take you higher, you have to ask yourself, "What kind of church am I attending?" If you're going to a church that either criticizes or doesn't teach on prosperity, you're making a huge mistake. You should have a pastor that's encouraging you in this area. You shouldn't have to struggle with attending the church or keeping your beliefs under wraps. In the same way that you choose your group of friends, you have to choose the church to which you belong.

I love healing. If I was looking for a home church and heard the pastor say, "How many of you know sickness can come from God and sometimes He can use it to teach us a lesson?" I'd be out of there! I won't travel on the road and leave my wife and daughter in that church. I refuse to have those things spoken over them and then wonder why they're battling illnesses. Instead, I've intentionally chose my home church where healing is preached. If my family isn't on the road with me, I have peace of mind knowing that they're in the company of people to whom I've aligned myself. It's the same with wealth. You can't grow rich sitting in a church where they glorify poverty.

I don't understand why people are so loyal to a church or a denomination. Pastor Lester Sumrall once said something that's stuck with me. He said that people are strange. They want the most recent, cutting-edge television or the latest car. On the other hand, when it comes to a church, they'll go to the same one their family's been attending for the last hundred years. I'm not encouraging you to swap out churches every five years, but if your church or denomination quits moving with God, then it's time to break company and find where the move of God is. I've made up my mind that I'm not sticking around some dead denomination or ministerial fellowship.

Ask yourself these important questions: Where do you go to church? Who do you hang around? Break away from the wrong people and begin to pursue those who call on the

Lord with pure hearts and love the blessing of God. There's a principle in the Scriptures that like spirits attract. For example, if you're a minister in a spiritually dead denomination and attend their minister's meetings, you'll find spiritually dead people. No spiritually alive people are going to places like that. You'll only meet failures and bums your whole life, which will be in no way a help to you. You end up longing for services to be over so you can drive home and get away from all the boredom. Is that any way to live?

When you get around people that are moving forward, you will constantly come across people that are inspirations. Proverbs 27:17 (NIV) says, **"As iron sharpens iron, so one person sharpens another."** God doesn't want you meeting losers all the time. If you pursue the blessing, you'll find other people who are pursuing the blessing. You will come in contact with winners and champions. They will sharpen you and you will sharpen them. You'll genuinely look forward to attending minister functions. Imagine if you sincerely looked forward to attending church because you were no longer going to a dead church – full of people who criticize anyone who is moving forward. Instead, you were attending a church where people love God and have decided they're going to overcome every obstacle that comes their way.

To those of you reading this who are single, did you ever think that the reason none of the guys or girls at your church interest you is because they are all spiritually dead? You may be unable to find someone because you're at a spiritually dead church. If you attend a church where people are striving to obtain the blessing of God, you're going to meet men and women who are overcomers. You can meet a bunch of backslidden people at a dead church and know it would be a mistake to marry any of them. Imagine if you were to attend a church and could meet men and women on fire for God that you could marry?

Choose carefully where you go to church. Choose wisely the ministerial fellowship you're a part of. Find people that are on fire for God. If you don't know of any good ministerial fellowships, I recommend Revival Ministries International Ministerial Association. I urge you, get to where the living reside.

Numbers chapters 13 and 14, tells the story of twelve spies that were sent to take the land that God had promised His children. Ten of the spies said the Israelites would be unable to take the land. The Bible says they spread their wicked report of unbelief amongst the people until they all began to cry. Unbelief is contagious. If you hang around anti-prosperity people, their unbelief is contagious. You may think it won't rub off on you, but what you don't realize, is that it already has.

Joshua and Caleb separated themselves from the ten unbelieving spies. In Numbers 14 they declared – we're able to take the country, to possess it from Jordan to the sea. And though there are giants in the land, if the Lord is with us, they are merely bread for us. We will defeat them with ease. After hearing this, the entire Hebrew camp spoke of stoning Joshua and Caleb to death. Sadly, not everyone is going to like when you say you're moving forward to take what God said is yours. When men said they were able to possess the blessing of God, people wanted to kill them. If you share what you've learned in this book with most people in the body of Christ they'd say, "Oh, one of those prosperity preachers. You need to be careful listening to that."

People hate when others advance beyond where they think you can go. When you progress ahead of them and display that you don't have to be small, they find it embarrassing. Rather than be embarrassed, or be teachable and learn, they attack the person that moved forward. Joshua and Caleb never went backwards. They had to break company with the people they had marched with for years. God rewarded Joshua and Caleb because of their actions. He gave them what they said they could have, while the other ten spies received what they themselves claimed.

In Numbers 14:26-28 God said that all the spies would die in the desert for their complaining. Who you hang around is going to affect what you believe, and what you believe determines what you say. The Bible says that death and life are in the power of the tongue (Proverbs 18:21). You can't believe and speak prosperity, while hanging around people that don't believe and speak poverty. Furthermore, break away from those type of people and join company with the right people.

You're already off to a great start by reading this book. Yet, it doesn't make up for going to a dead church or one that doesn't believe in prosperity. Don't fall into the trap of trying to move forward surrounded by the dead. You're alive! God's made you alive and quickened you by His Spirit. If you have to leave places you've been for years, do it! There's a whole other camp waiting for you, comprised of living people, looking to take ground for the kingdom of God. It will cause your life to become the most enjoyable it's ever been and you'll finish your race well, in Jesus' name!

Chapter 4

Building God's Word
Into Your Spirit-Man

"I promise you what I promised Moses: 'Wherever you set your foot, you will be on land I have given you – from the Negev wilderness in the south to the Lebanon mountains in the north, from the Euphrates River in the east to the Mediterranean Sea in the west, including all the land of the Hittites. No one will be able to stand against you as long as you live. For I will be with you as I was with Moses. I will not fail you or abandon you. Be strong and courageous, for you are the one who will lead these people to possess all the land I swore to their ancestors I would give them. Be strong and very courageous. Be careful to obey all the instructions Moses gave you. Do not deviate from them, turning either to the right or to the left. Then you will be successful in everything you do. Study this Book of Instruction continually. Meditate on it day and night so you will be sure to obey everything written in it. Only then will you prosper and succeed in all you do."

JOSHUA 1:3-8

When God passed the baton from Moses to Joshua, God gave Joshua the key to success. The key was to keep God's Word before him and to not deviate from any of His instructions. A key to prosperity is keeping God's Word before you and meditating on it day and night. Meditation is quality thought on what you've just read. Learn to sit quietly and allow the Lord to speak to you by His Spirit on how to apply what you've just read or heard to your life.

Romans 10:17 (NKJV) says, **"So then faith comes by hearing, and hearing by the word of God."** Faith is produced from hearing the Word of God preached, not just reading it. The one thing that changed my life from all standpoints, including a financial standpoint, was when the Lord first spoke to me to start offering two services a day rather than just one evening service. Along with that, I felt God speak to me that if I didn't increase my study time and plant more of God's Word in my spirit, I would become dry and run out of material. I wouldn't have enough to preach. I began to listen to great men of God such as Bishop Oyedepo, Pastor Adeboye, Matthew Ashimolowo, T.L. Osborn, Kenneth Hagin, and Lester Sumrall for roughly an hour a day. Locate people who have the gifts you want and listen to them preach. Subsequently, what's in their spirit will get into your spirit.

Ezekiel 2:2 (KJV) says, **"And the spirit entered into me when he spake unto me..."** Preaching is a great form of impartation. Although the laying on of hands is an impartation, listening to preaching will enhance any impact the laying on of hands may have. If you take someone who listens to a specific preacher every day for a year and compare them with someone who simply experienced the laying on of hands; the person that listened to the preaching is going to receive a significantly greater impartation. For example, Bishop Oyedepo never had the opportunity to have Kenneth Hagin lay hands on him, but he tells about a dramatic encounter he had when he came to Tulsa, Oklahoma to hear Brother Hagin preach. He had a life-changing encounter with God through the preaching of His Word. Similar to how Samuel encountered God by His Word in the Bible (1 Samuel 3:21).

People often underestimate the preaching of the Word. They think we should just skip over it and move onto prayer. Some churches will give altar calls to pray for the sick before there has been any preaching. In reality, the preaching of God's Word is the highest thing. God honors His Word above His name. It's a drastic means of impartation for the listener. When you listen to people preach, there's an unction of the Holy Ghost on what they're saying. The Bible says that faith comes by hearing God's Word (Romans 10:17). Your life is going to be defined by the faith that you carry. Faith is not merely a belief system. Faith is not just saying, "I'm an Episcopal" or "I'm a Methodist." Faith is raw spiritual power, a substance that makes you a commander in life.

When you believe, faith causes all things to become possible. And all things are possible for the one who believes. Then how can you increase your faith? You won't find any scriptures in the Bible on building faith by listening to praise and worship music. You can't pray, "Lord increase my faith." If you did, the answer would be for you to use the means by which God instructed you to produce faith – by hearing the Word of God.

Magalis, on my staff at Revival Today, essentially gave herself a Masters in Broadcasting by watching online tutorials on how to build our radio station from scratch.

Faith allows solutions to those who are having a problem; where the Word of God is built into their spirit rather than someone needing prayer. They can access the raw power of God for themselves through the preaching of God's Word.

The week when we received a 1 million dollar offering, finances had been heavily weighing on my mind. When we started our ministry a few years ago, we believed God for $3,000 dollars a month to sustain the ministry and ourselves. As the ministry started to grow, I hired other people to handle our finances. After that, I didn't realize the rapid extent to which our ministry was growing. A couple of weeks before receiving the 1 million dollar offering, I met with our ministry's Board of Directors and discovered we needed $2.4 million to come in that year to break even. In order to make that happen, I calculated that we'd need $50,000 dollars to come in each week.

In the past I would shout, jump, and testify to everyone I saw when $50,000 dollars came in within one week. Today, I would just roll into the next week with no pressure or worry. However, our finances at that point began weighing on my mind. Rather than just sit around worried, wondering how it would happen, I decided to build God's Word into my spirit. I already knew a lot about prosperity; however, if I needed to go to another level financially, then I needed to build what God's Word said about finances into my spirit. God didn't tell Joshua, "Study the Bible for a little while, keep it before you for a bit, and when you feel like you have a good grasp on it, stop studying." He told Joshua that the key to prospering in everything is to keep the Word of God ever before you, meditating on it every day and every night (Joshua 1:8).

During my time in Finland, I was able to get a hold of Dr. Fred Price's sermons on prosperity. Dr. Fred Price built the Crenshaw Friendship Christian Center, which was a 30 million dollar project paid for in cash. Dr. Price was able to pay 30 million dollars in cash by pastoring revelation and the power of God's Word. He helped people to prosper. I listened to his sermons from the time he was pushing to build the center God had instructed him to construct. The 30 million in cash came from his church, made up of poor or formally poor inner-city people that had begun to prosper because of what he preached. I built what Dr. Fred Price preached into my spirit. Moreover, I knew it wasn't by chance that we received the million dollar gift at the end of the week. Adalis and I had built what Dr. Fred Price preached into our spirits that entire week.

When you run into problems in life, it's usually an indicator of a place you've failed to build the Word of God strong in your life. Psalms 91:4 says, **"He will cover you with his feathers. He will shelter you with his wings. His faithful promises are your armor and protection."** You don't just have an automatic shield of faith. Your shield of faith is built by you diving into the Word of God in specific areas. You can be a master on prosperity and know nothing about healing. You can't honestly believe God's sovereign and question if He wants you sick. You'll have a gaping hole in your shield of faith where sickness can come and go as it pleases.

"**If you explain these things to the brothers and sisters, Timothy, you will be a worthy servant of Christ Jesus, one who is nourished by the message of faith and the good teaching you have followed. Do not waste time arguing over godless ideas and old wives' tales. Instead, train yourself to be godly. Physical training is good, but training for godliness is much better, promising benefits in this life and in the life to come... Teach these things and insist that everyone learn them. Don't let anyone think less of you because you are young. Be an example to all believers in what you say, in the way you live, in your love, your faith, and your purity. Until I get there, focus on reading the Scriptures to the church, encouraging the believers, and teaching them. Do not neglect the spiritual gift you received through the prophecy spoken over you when the elders of the church laid their hands on you. Give your complete attention to these matters. Throw yourself into your tasks so that everyone will see your progress.**"

1 TIMOTHY 4:6-8; 11-15

1 Timothy 4:15 in the *King James Version* reads, "**Meditate on these things; give thyself wholly to them; that thy profiting may appear unto all.**" Throughout the passage, Paul speaks about devoting yourself to the Scriptures and applying the Word of God. Then, he says, your profit will appear unto all. The Word of God will produce an effect in your life that other people will be able to see. What you build into your spirit through the Word of God will appear unto all. The fact that you walk in a high level of health will become apparent to people, and they'll

begin to ask what your secret is? How come you're always strong? How come you're never tired? People will begin to notice; it's a profiting that appears unto everyone.

Romans 1:16 says, **"For I am not ashamed of this Good News about Christ. It is the power of God at work, saving everyone who believes..."** When someone is sick all the time, there is a deficiency in his or her knowledge on the subject of healing. The Bible says the entrance of His words give light (Psalms 119:130). It's impossible to invest the Word of God into your spirit in any area and not experience an evident breaking forth of supernatural light. When you begin to build the revelation of divine healing into your spirit, you'll hit a point where there will be a breaking forth of that light; healing begins to manifest, not only in your own body, but in the bodies of those around you.

Hebrews 6:12 (KJV) says, **"[Be] followers of them who through faith and patience inherit the promises [of God]."** I challenge you to find people that are masters in the area where you want to see improvement. Whether its health, finances, joy, peace, etc. Find people that carry an anointing in that area. For example, if you're depressed, don't just put on a happy movie or go out and do something fun. Instead, start listening to Rodney Howard-Browne day and night. Listen to his messages because he carries joy. There's no way you can listen to him and stay depressed. The Word of God on joy will come into your spirit. For finances, listen to Bishop Oyedepo and Pastor Adeboye. Bishop Oyedepo and Pastor Adeboye are like a one-stop shop because in addition to finances, they offer some of the best preaching on healing I've ever heard.

Research and locate people that carry the anointing on their preaching in the area you want to build up. Listen to T.L. Osborn for healing. Dig up resources on healing from people that carry a powerful healing anointing. They carry such a powerful anointing due to their understanding of the Word of God. Listen to Kenneth Hagin's messages on faith and prosperity. All of the people's messages I've mentioned can be easily accessed through YouTube. Use my 24-hour radio station to build your spirit-man – that's what it's there for.

Take time to build your spirit-man, especially if you know you're under attack or have a problem. I took a week and listened to Dr. Fred Price's revelation on prosperity for at least two hours a day. I supernaturally received more that week than in the history of our ministry. It was a product of building God's Word into my spirit in the area that I wanted to see breakthrough. Build God's Word into your spirit every day in whatever area you want to see breakthrough.

Here are books that I believe every Christian should read that cover the main areas of life where Satan attacks:

1. *The Believer's Authority* by Kenneth Hagin
2. *Healing the Sick* by T.L. Osborn
3. *Understanding Financial Prosperity* by Bishop David Oyedepo
4. *Exploits in Ministry* by Bishop David Oyedepo
5. *This Present Glory* by Dr. Rodney Howard-Browne
6. *Gifts and Ministries of the Holy Spirit* by Dr. Lester Sumrall

The more you build faith into your spirit, the more you become an unstoppable force on this earth. That's where you're headed today, in Jesus' name.

Chapter 5

Godliness

"Oh, the joys of those who do not follow the advice of the wicked, or stand around with sinners, or join in with mockers. But they delight in the law of the LORD, meditating on it day and night. They are like trees planted along the riverbank, bearing fruit each season. Their leaves never wither, and they prosper in all they do."

PSALMS 1:1-3

Godliness ensures greatness. Godliness by itself, however, will not make you wealthy. Avoiding alcohol, not committing adultery, and being kind alone, doesn't bring any financial reward. All the principles in this book must be active in your life.

Godliness is the platform that you stand on for God to bless you. If you're on the platform of wickedness, God can't bless you. If you're standing on the platform of godliness, you are now bless-able. Godliness by itself won't make you wealthy, but you'll be standing in a place that allows all of these principles to work.

Wickedness will guarantee your inability to keep the money you earn. I could write about various musicians and athletes celebrated as the richest people alive when I was younger, who are now in bankruptcy. How does an athlete blow through $169 million dollars in nine years? I'll tell you how, by paying child support for ten children to nine different women. Wickedness not only opens a door to hell, it eats at your money. Holy living allows you to keep the wealth that's produced from what God has called you to do. It enables you to operate in the blessing of God.

If you live a sinful life, it's like having a basket with holes. You can earn a lot, but all the money drifts out of it. If you live the way God has instructed, you have a basket without holes, and are able to retain the blessing of God.

Do you know how easy it is to grow your wealth when you don't have to divide it every few years after a divorce, or give it to an ex-girlfriend who sues you for every penny? It's incredibly easy to retain the blessing of God. I have never had to spend money on bail or DUI lawyers. I've never had to spend money to get my wife out of a methadone clinic. Anything you do to engage in a worldly, godless lifestyle will cost you money. When you live the way God has told you to live, you're creating a lifestyle to preserve your blessings.

"So I say, let the Holy Spirit guide your lives. Then you won't be doing what your sinful nature craves. The sinful nature wants to do evil, which is just the opposite of what the Spirit wants. And the Spirit gives us desires that are the opposite of what the sinful nature desires. These two forces are constantly fighting each other, so you are not free to carry out your good intentions. But when you are directed by the Spirit, you are not under obligation to the law of Moses. When you follow the

desires of your sinful nature, the results are very clear: sexual immorality, impurity, lustful pleasures, idolatry, sorcery, hostility, quarreling, jealousy, outbursts of anger, selfish ambition, dissension, division, envy, drunkenness, wild parties, and other sins like these. Let me tell you again, as I have before, that anyone living that sort of life will not inherit the Kingdom of God."

GALATIANS 5:16-21

Godliness Ensures Your Conduct Lines Up with God's Commands

You can't just hope that God will make you godly. It's your responsibility. The Bible says to get rid of every evil thing lurking within you (Colossians 3:5). God has given you the power to take care of it.

Godliness is taking personal responsibility to ensure your conduct lines up with God's commands. Some people try to preach that godliness is an ethereal thing. They think, "Because I've given my life to Jesus Christ, I've been made right with God – regardless of what my actions may show." No, your actions prove what is on the inside of your heart. You know a tree by its fruit so you know a person by their actions (Matthew 7:20). If your actions are unholy and wickedness is a part of your lifestyle, you don't possess a godly heart. Godly hearts do not produce wickedness.

In John 15:5 Jesus says, **"Yes, I am the vine; you are the branches..."** The following verse says that branches that don't produce fruit **"... are gathered into a pile to be burned"** (John 15:6). You can be connected to Christ initially, but your ungodly conduct can cause you to be cut off and thrown into the fire. Only a fool would get saved and then not be concerned with how he or she lives.

"Don't you realize that in a race everyone runs, but only one person gets the prize? So run to win! All athletes are disciplined in their training. They do it to win a prize that will fade away, but we do it for an eternal prize. So I run with purpose in every step. I am not just shadowboxing. I discipline my body like an athlete, training it to do what it should. Otherwise, I fear that after preaching to others I myself might be disqualified."

1 CORINTHIANS 9:24-27

Wise people concern themselves with how they live every single day. They pray, "Lord, point out anything in me that offends you so I can make it right." Keep a close watch on your lifestyle. Backsliding is never sudden; it's a slow, steady leak. Examine your life daily and ask yourself: What am I allowing into my life? What have I started to watch? What have I started to listen to? Where am I starting to go? Am I drifting closer to the plan of God or farther away? If you take care of that every day, you'll never backslide or miss heaven.

An evil tree produces evil fruit. A rotten tree produces rotten fruit. If your heart has been transformed, the proof will be in your actions. You have to take responsibility to ensure your conduct lines up with God's commands.

Godliness Has No Room for Alcohol

The Bible says no drunkard will enter the Kingdom of Heaven (1 Corinthians 6:10). You might debate that a beer is fine as long as you don't get drunk. But do you really want to ride the line and find out on Judgment Day if God considers getting a buzz drunk?

The approach shouldn't be, "Now I can live any way I want, God's grace will cover it." Galatians 5:21 refers to avoiding alcohol. As a reminder, Galatians is in the New Testament, not the Old Testament. Paul, who was the author of the message of grace, wrote Galatians. He didn't have a poor understanding of grace. He's writing this letter to a church he's already preached to. This isn't an open letter for whatever sinners are passing by. It was written to Christians, people who had already given their lives to the Lord.

People claim that it doesn't say anywhere in the Bible that you can't drink, it only says you can't get drunk. That's actually not true. The parents of both Samson and John the Baptist were given special direction from heaven to never let alcohol touch their son's lips. The command wasn't, "Don't let them get drunk." The command was to never let alcohol touch their lips (Judges 13:4, 7, 14; Luke 1:15). Why? Because they were set apart for a special work to be used by the Holy Spirit. There's a differentiation between the Holy Spirit and the spirit of alcohol, which is literally called "spirits." That alone should tell you to stay away from it.

The New Testament says not to be drunk with wine for it will ruin your life, but to instead be filled with the Holy Spirit (Ephesians 5:18). Notice it doesn't say, "drink and be filled with the Holy Spirit." You have to make a choice. You are either going to be a drinker or someone filled with and used by the Holy Spirit. Godliness has no room for drunkenness.

I've seen childhood church friends and Bible school peers buy into the modern message that it's okay to drink and dabble in the likes. They have gone nowhere. I also have friends that were called into the ministry and started drinking. They've been trying to plant a church for three years, but can't seem to get anything moving. After a period of time, you'd expect people to realize that God's hand isn't on what they're doing. It's as if God doesn't want them spreading their reckless beliefs to other people.

I have never had one drop of alcohol. On my 21st birthday, I preached in Massachusetts. I don't do stupid things like party and drink all night. I am set apart to God. Your life has to be separated from the wicked and set apart to God. You can't do everything people in the world do and expect to have a different life than theirs. Separating yourself unto God means separating yourself from alcohol.

Isn't it amazing that all the revivals that swept through England, Wales, and the United States shut down all the bars? That was a natural result of the revivals. Who are these irresponsible preachers that tell people that it's okay to drink? It's a devil.

Godliness Has No Room for Wild Parties

I'm not talking about having no room for throwing a birthday party; I'm talking about *wild parties*. The world is full of them – Miami, New York City, Los Angeles, Las Vegas. Every city in the world has them, and they're always glamorized in the media. Paul warned against it 2,000 years ago, it's nothing new.

You can't participate in wild parties and live a godly life. I believe anyone reading this understands what wild parties entail – girls in provocative clothing, guys with their clothes unbuttoned too far, everyone looking to drink, loud music that encourages people to hook up for the night. Wild parties are breeding grounds for sexual immorality.

Godliness Has No Room for Sexual Immorality

Paul said that no sexually immoral person will enter the Kingdom of God (1 Corinthians 6:9). What's sexual immorality? Any sex, gay or straight, outside of marriage. Since there is no such thing as gay marriage according to God, all homosexuality is sexual immorality.

If you live with someone, you're sleeping with them. I was preaching at a church and a couple in their mid-twenties approached me afterwards to talk. They said they'd heard me preach that it was wrong to live with someone of the opposite sex if you're not married. They alleged that they live together but don't sleep together, so is it still wrong?

I followed up by saying, "I'm a minister of the Gospel of the Lord Jesus Christ. I'm a servant of God. We are standing at the altar of God. I'm going to have you say that one more time, and if it's not true and you do sleep together, I'm going to have God strike you dead on the spot. Go ahead and say it again." They quickly responded, "Okay, we sleep together sometimes." Of course they did! He didn't have a girl move in because he needed a partner to play Scrabble!

I can't even blame the modern generation. Not only did their parents probably do the same thing, but also possibly badmouthed marriage to their children – even Christian parents! They tell their kids, "You need to be careful. You need to make sure you have a Master's Degree first. You need to have a good career before you get married." Is it any wonder why Christians aren't getting married until they're thirty-eight years old? In the same manner, many choose not to have any children because their parents have scared them out of the idea. It's all rooted in how decried and bemoaned marriage has become!

Marriage is not something that subtracts from life. Marriage benefits your life! Proverbs 18:22 (NKJV) says, **"He who finds a wife finds a good thing, and obtains favor from the Lord."**

"Finds a good thing" – not a ball and chain.

"Obtains favor from the Lord" – not hardship.

God created marriage as a structure to facilitate blessing. You have to participate in it if you're going to have that blessing. My wife Adalis is not a detriment to my life nor has she been a ball and chain. She's been a jet engine that God placed alongside me to get me to my destiny. It's much better with her than without her.

Sexual immorality will cost you; just watch any daytime court show. It's all centered on people who moved in together or slept with each other, and half of them don't know who their baby's daddy is.

You have to be sexually pure if you're going to live a godly lifestyle. I know not everyone is privileged to grow up in a family like mine. My dad is a preacher and my mother is a Holy Spirit filled woman who graduated from Bible College. The first woman I slept with was my wife on our wedding night. They try to tell you that no one lives like that anymore. I went through high school without kissing anyone. I went to Bible College and worked a secular job, yet I never went to a bar. I never hooked up with a girl. I never had an "off night" where I made a mistake and slept with someone and had to repent.

You can live a holy life! Don't let any devil tell you otherwise. It's imperative that you live a holy life if you're going to walk in the blessing of God. To live a holy life, specific things have to be removed from your life: drunkenness, wild parties, sexual immorality and lastly, outbursts of anger.

Godliness Has No Room for Outbursts of Anger

Think of all the celebrities in the last year that lost their income and went to jail because of an outburst of anger. One national football player shot someone to death and will be in jail for the rest of his life. Not only did he walk away from millions of dollars, he walked away from freedom. No one will see him again.

You have to check your anger. As strict as laws are now, you can't lash out and lose your temper. This isn't the "Wild West" where you can duke it out with anyone who makes you angry. You can lose everything that God gave you in a moment of anger. In a split second you can punch someone, get arrested for assault, spend hundreds of thousands of dollars on legal fees to stay out of prison, possibly lose money in a settlement, and potentially go to jail – where you can't make any money.

Rid yourself of angry outbursts. If you're a man, don't consider a violent temper the mark of being a man. It doesn't mean you're macho or have testosterone. Ecclesiastes 7:9 (NKJV) says, **"Do not hasten in your spirit to be angry, for anger rests in the bosom of fools."** People will actually brag about something that the Bible says marks them as a fool.

"I have a temper. You don't want to get me mad."

"I'm Irish; I have a temper."

"I'm Dominican; I have a temper."

"I'm Italian; I have a temper."

"I'm Puerto Rican; I have a temper."

Quit blaming stuff on your nationality. People do the same thing when it comes to drinking:

"We drink; we're Irish."

"We drink; we're Italian."

"We drink; we're French."

"We drink; we're Australian."

I received an invitation to preach in another country and was asked to avoid preaching on alcohol because it was part of the culture. I said, "Yes, unlike the country I live in, America, where nobody touches alcohol."

Quit making allowances for your behavior based on your culture. Realize that when you were born again, God gave you the power to rise above your culture and live a different lifestyle than the world's.

A Life of Unending Increase

"Oh, the joys of those who do not follow the advice of the wicked, or stand around with sinners, or join in with mockers. But they delight in the law of the LORD, meditating on it day and night. They are like trees planted along the riverbank, bearing fruit each season. Their leaves never wither, and they prosper in all they do."

PSALMS 1:1-3

Let's takes a closer look at this scripture in order to expound on the three things a godly life entails:

Bear Fruit in Every Season

That means there are no "down seasons" for the godly man. I can't get with modern Charismatic Christianity, where everyone is continually waiting for their season. Sometimes you'll hear Christians say, "I'm telling you a season of increase is coming to the body of Christ." I don't know what body of Christ you're a part of but if you're in the actual body of Christ and live a godly life, then you don't just have a season of increase. The Bible says that you'll increase in each season and bring forth fruit.

Leaves Never Wither

That means no setbacks. The last setback you saw will be the last one you will ever see. Nothing is permitted to make your leaves wither. Nothing is permitted to keep you from bearing fruit. Every attack of the devil, plot of the government, plan by man or Satan; anything to keep you poor or take away your wealth, will be struck down for your sake.

This passage of scripture also talks about physical vibrancy. If your body begins to wither then you can't produce wealth nor enjoy the wealth you've produced. God said you'll never wither, you'll be vibrant, and you'll produce fruit every day. That's your inheritance. Your leaves will never wither. **"Surely goodness and mercy shall follow me all the days of my life: and I will dwell in the house of the Lord forever"** (Psalms 23:6, KJV). The Bible says as your days, so shall your strength be (Deuteronomy 33:25).

Prosper in All You Do

That means everything the Lord leads you to do, He has led you to in order to prosper. Until you get that in your spirit, you'll be open to failure. I've lost track of the number of pastors who have small churches that say, "Well I guess I'm like Jeremiah. He never had one convert throughout his whole ministry." No, you are not Jeremiah. You're filled with the Holy Ghost and you are in the New Covenant. In the book of Acts, you won't come across a time where Christians were called to go somewhere, and there were no salvations. They were fruitful; they prospered in everything they did.

God didn't have you start a business to try and test your patience. He put you in that business to prosper you. The godly prosper in everything they do. They don't lose. They don't break even. They bring profit. **"Thus says the Lord, your Redeemer, the Holy One of Israel: 'I am the Lord your God, Who teaches you to profit, Who leads you by the way you should go'"** (Isaiah 48:17, NKJV).

When you choose to live a godly life, it ensures a life of godly increases. What if you've already messed up? What if it's too late? What if you've already slept around? 2 Corinthians 5:17 says, **"... that anyone who belongs to Christ has become a new person. The old life is gone; a new life has begun!"** God never leads into stagnation, He leads into prosperity. Godliness ensures you will enjoy that prosperity.

"But God's truth stands firm like a foundation stone with this inscription: 'The Lord knows those who are his,' and 'All who belong to the LORD must turn away from evil.' In a wealthy home some utensils are made of gold and silver, and some are made of wood and clay. The expensive utensils are used for special occasions, and the cheap ones are for everyday use. If you keep yourself pure, you will be a special utensil for honorable use. Your life will be clean, and you will be ready for the Master to use you for every good work. Run from anything that stimulates youthful lusts. Instead, pursue righteous living, faithfulness, love, and peace. Enjoy the

companionship of those who call on the Lord with pure hearts."

2 TIMOTHY 2:19-22

How do you live in accordance with this Scripture? You do it by enjoying the companionship of those who call on the Lord with pure hearts. You're never going to live a godly life when your five closest friends are lukewarm Christians. Separate yourself from wicked and lukewarm people and enjoy the companionship of those who are equally yoked with you and pursuing righteousness.

You can't move forward with God when you're hanging around people who are content with where they are or are following after the world. There has to be a separation in your life.

When you keep yourself pure you become a special utensil in God's drawer, set apart for a special work. When you have everyday company over your house, your mother uses the plastic plates and utensils. If your parents' friends are coming over, they use the good plates and utensils. Then there's the China cabinet, which has the plates reserved for royalty. It has fine dishes, forks, a teapot, and tea set. It was in my parents' home growing up and none of the items were ever brought out. They were set apart for a special work. They were never deemed worthy for common use.

Did you know God has a chest of drawers like that? God has a special drawer for special utensils that are set apart for a special work. If you want to be set apart, high above all the nations of the world, it starts by setting yourself apart from wickedness and pursuing righteous living. When you do that, it ensures that God will set you apart for a special work. It's not just by chance, it's guaranteed.

The first directive is to run from anything that stimulates youthful lusts (2 Timothy 2:19). In your youth, you can choose whether you're going to sleep around and do what everyone else does, or flee youthful lusts and live a life that is set apart for God.

Look at the life of Joseph. Joseph could have thrown away his entire destiny by sleeping with Potiphar's wife. When she begged him to sleep with her, his response wasn't simply, "No, you're married. Get a divorce first." He said, "… **How could I do such a wicked thing? It would be a great sin against God**" (Genesis 39:9).

Joseph had separated himself to God. He refused to violate the covenant. Afterwards, it looked as if he was going nowhere. In fact, Joseph was put in prison after he made that choice. Later on, however, his decision to live pure and righteously led him to become Prime Minister of the greatest nation on earth.

Don't allow this chapter to be a condemning one. Use it to make your mind up today to be done with sin. Say goodbye to the pleasures of sin and worldly living. Remember, God didn't say, "If you are far from me, don't consider coming back!" He said, "… **Return to me, and I will return to you…**" (Zechariah 1:3). Give yourself completely to God and commit to keep that vow from this day forward. That same divine selection comes on you today, in the name of Jesus Christ. I declare you set apart for a special work as you separate yourself from anything that would lead you into sin and take you out of the will of God. Today, as you return to God, God returns to you. Make it your vow, not just an attempt. Make your life an undying commitment to holy living and watch the power of God manifest in your life. You'll be set apart for your generation.

Chapter 6

Giving

"... 'You have cheated me of the tithes and offerings due to me. You are under a curse, for your whole nation has been cheating me. Bring all the tithes into the storehouse so there will be enough food in my Temple. If you do,' says the LORD of Heaven's Armies, 'I will open the windows of heaven for you. I will pour out a blessing so great you won't have enough room to take it in! Try it! Put me to the test! Your crops will be abundant, for I will guard them from insects and disease. Your grapes will not fall from the vine before they are ripe,' says the LORD of Heaven's Armies. 'Then all nations will call you blessed, for your land will be such a delight,' says the LORD of Heaven's Armies."

MALACHI 3:8-12

People claim that tithing is under the Old Covenant and thus, doesn't apply to us today. But tithing existed before the Law was ever created. Abraham tithed before the Law and Abraham existed before Moses. **"What sorrow awaits you teachers of religious law and you Pharisees. Hypocrites! For you are careful to tithe even the tiniest income from your herb gardens, but you ignore the**

75

more important aspects of the law – justice, mercy, and faith. You should tithe, yes, but do not neglect the more important things" (Matthew 23:23).

Note that it says, "You should tithe, yes." Which in the original language means, "You should tithe, yes." Tithing was not just part of the Law or the Old Covenant. Jesus brought it into the New Covenant. Abraham tithed before there was a Law or Old Covenant. Cain and Abel gave offerings to God in early Genesis along with Adam and Eve.

The Bible says that no one should ever appear before God without a gift (Deuteronomy 16:16). I know this may sound like a foreign religion to American Christians who have been told by pastors: "Don't feel any compulsion to give. You don't have to give this morning. If you're a first-time visitor, just let that offering plate pass you by." All people do is apologize for offerings. That's why churches, by and large, don't enjoy any resources. It takes them twenty-five years to do something that a secular corporation can do in eight to ten months.

If you stand against any doctrine, you'll never enjoy the blessing of it. Likewise, any doctrine you stand on will be manifested in your life. I've always stood up for divine healing and it's always stood up for me. When I preached on it during the infancy of my ministry, it caused ministers to get upset and yell, declaring they'd never invite me back. My family has always enjoyed great health because I've always stood on the promise of divine healing.

The last time I saw a doctor was when I had to in order to travel to the Democratic Republic of Congo to preach. I wasn't sick. I haven't been treated for a sickness by any human in a long, long time. Before the trip to the Democratic Republic of Congo, I went for a physical to play ice hockey in high school. Prior to that I went to the doctor as a child when my mother and father would take me and I had no say in the matter.

In the same way, I've always taken a stand for giving. The Bible mentions giving 50 percent more times than healing. Nonetheless, preachers don't want to talk about giving and Christians storm out when they do. When I spoke on giving at one of my meetings, a man stormed out and yelled at my wife, "This is ridiculous!" I wish I could say that his reaction was uncommon.

What many fail to recognize is that the last thing the devil wants is for believers to be rich. People that have wealth have the ability to sway policy and law making. They determine who owns land. As long as the devil can keep his crowd rich they'll continue to have vast influence. Churches then have to be built someplace that requires a compass and an Indian guide to find. Without money, it's impossible to have any good property in the center of a bustling town. If the only way the church can have money is by getting loans, the devil and his crowd will continue to get rich off us, since borrowing from the wicked is our only option.

I firmly believe with all my heart that God's going to raise up a new generation of believers that are not going to be poor. They will walk in the redemptive wealth that was paid for by Jesus. Jesus paid too high a price on the cross for us to be poor. **"You know the generous grace of our Lord Jesus Christ. Though he was rich, yet for your sakes he became poor, so that by his poverty he could make you rich"** (2 Corinthians 8:9).

Jesus didn't come to simply meet your needs. He came to make you rich. Part of what Christ did in redemption was to make you wealthy. God has a desire for you to walk in wealth. About 2,000 Scriptures deal with wealth, stewardship, and God's blessing on your finances. God desires that for you! There are principles, however, that you have to engage to enjoy it – and giving is one of those.

When one gentleman at a church put $1.1 million dollars in the offering, it opened a window of heaven over our ministry. Which otherwise, would've taken ten years to receive. It came in one night, from one church, and it wasn't a mega or famous church. It was a recently established church that was and continues to be blessed by God.

When God opens the windows of heaven over your life neither the government nor recession can be of any hindrance. When the windows of heaven come open over your life, the earth loses its power to keep you poor. I want you to understand that there are two sides of the giving coin. On one side, there are churches that don't give anything. On the opposite side, are churches that beat giving to death. These churches take three or four offerings every Sunday: Building fund, Sunday school, bless the Pastor, and the list goes on and on. They preach as if giving is the only key to blessing. While it is a principle, it's one of the many types of giving I'll share in this chapter.

There's a vast variety of sports under the larger umbrella of sports in general. Each sport has its own set of rules. In the same way, the Bible has different kinds of giving. There are seven types of giving in the Bible. I want you to understand them because you can't yield results without an understanding.

When you read through these types of giving, you'll realize that you've only been doing three of them. Do all of them! When you do, you'll notice that there's a real blessing attached to giving, just as there's a real curse for withholding what's due to God. God didn't say, "Return to me and I won't be angry anymore." He said if you return to me in the tithes and the offering, see if I won't open the windows of heaven and pour you out a blessing that is so great, you won't have room enough to take it all in. That sounds like a good deal to me!

The following are the seven types of giving that every believer should be engaging in: tithe, offering, first fruits, almsgiving, sacrificial giving, honoring a man of God, and partnering with a traveling ministry.

Tithe

"'Bring all the tithes into the storehouse so there will be enough food in my Temple. If you do,' says the LORD of Heaven's Armies, 'I will open the windows of heaven for you. I will pour out a blessing so great you won't have enough room to take it in! Try it! Put me to the test!'"

MALACHI 3:10

The tithe is 10% of your gross income – not your net income or what's left after paying your bills. The tithe is 10% off the top. It's not just something you give to God; it belongs to God. If you withhold it, you're stealing from God. It's a sin to not tithe. A non-tither can never be blessed. If you think you're too smart to tithe, you're too dumb to prosper.

You need to decide if you'd rather have 90% of your income blessed or 100% of it cursed. People say they can't afford to tithe, but the reality is that you can't afford not to tithe! You're going to pay your tithe somewhere. Either you'll bring your tithe to the Lord with joy or you're going to pay it with interest somewhere else.

People that don't tithe always have something going wrong. That's not the case for my family, everything in our home lasts. The parts on our vehicles last. We don't have things breaking down all the time and eating up our money. Why? Because God said part of the blessing for tithing is that He rebukes the Devourer for your sake. He won't allow things to eat at your money. This principle also applies to your health. If you have to pay for treatments and hospital bills, your health can eat at your money. I believe that tithing puts a shield around the devil's ability to attack your body.

The Bible says that he that is unfaithful in the small things will be unfaithful in everything (Luke 16:10). If you can't follow God on something as simple as giving Him a dime of every dollar He gives you, you'll never prosper. Look at it this way, 100% of every dollar you make belongs to God and He's only asking for 10%. Without God, there's no check. Not only does everything you make come from God, but so does the hand that writes the check, the eye that looks at the check, and the brain that calculates the 10% tithe. God only asks for 10% of it back. When you give it, He opens the windows of heaven over your life.

One time I was on a panel with some ministers who said if you earned $1,500 dollars you should consider rounding up your tithe to $200. You can't round up the tithe; it's a fixed 10%. It's not that hard, it's a set amount. God said it, you can't alter it. You can't double tithe. You can't reverse tithe. The tithe belongs to the Lord and the tithe is 10%. If you give 7% you might as well give zero. If God tells you to build an ark and you build a canoe, you're going to drown. You can't negotiate the tithe down.

I'm shocked by how many ministers group all giving under tithing. There are rules for certain sports that don't work in other sports. If you try to play football by the rules of baseball, you're going to get thrown off the field.

Offering

"Remember this – a farmer who plants only a few seeds will get a small crop. But the one who plants generously will get a generous crop. You must each decide in your heart how much to give. And don't give reluctantly or in response to pressure. 'For God loves a person who gives cheerfully.' And God will generously provide all you need. Then you will always have everything you need and plenty left over to share with others."

2 CORINTHIANS 9:6-8

Most people conglomerate all their giving under "tithes." You'll hear people say that they tithe 20%. You can't tithe 20%, tithe means tenth. People say they reverse tithe by keeping 10% and giving 90% to God. No, you can only tithe 10%. But giving doesn't stop at the tithe, you have to give above the tithe, as it says in Malachi, you have cheated me of the tithes *and* offerings. The tithe is a fixed amount determined by God. While on the other hand, you decide the offering.

What is an offering? An offering is what you give above the tithe to honor God. You need to consider various factors when you decide how much to give. The whole book of Malachi is spent rebuking people for not giving. Giving clearly matters to God. You're to give out of love. You don't give because a ministry is doing a telethon and says there's seven minutes left for the matching challenge. Don't give reluctantly or in response to pressure, give with joy.

"You have shown contempt by offering defiled sacrifices on my altar. Then you ask, 'How have we defiled the sacrifices?' 'You defile them by saying the altar of the LORD deserves no respect. When you give blind animals as sacrifices, isn't that wrong? And isn't it wrong to offer animals that are crippled and diseased? Try giving gifts like that to your governor, and see how pleased he is!' says the LORD of Heaven's Armies. 'Go ahead, beg God to be merciful to you! But when you bring that kind of offering, why should he show you any favor at all?' asks the LORD of Heaven's Armies. 'How I wish one of you would shut the Temple doors so that these worthless sacrifices could not be offered! I am not pleased with you,' says the LORD of Heaven's Armies, 'and I will not accept your offerings.'"

MALACHI 1:7-10

God doesn't accept every offering. Many poor people in the body of Christ give in every offering, but they've never given an offering that God's accepted. In Malachi, God asks them to close the doors of the Temple so he wouldn't have to look at the garbage they were bringing Him (that's my translation). What people were giving God was actually irritating Him. Not only was He not receiving it, He was angry! God said if you brought a person what you're trying to bring to me, people would be angry.

Do you think putting loose coins in the offering bucket is going to move God? You couldn't even buy something at McDonald's with that amount. I didn't even put change in the offering when I was five years old. I would make the adult I was with give me at least a dollar bill to put in the offering. People putting in 38-cents or fishing through their purse for some pennies and dimes have grown to be customary in the church. They drop it in the offering, giving God their trash and expect His treasure in return. God said the offering has to be something that's worthy of your honor for Him. If it doesn't move you, it won't move God. The offering should represent your heart.

Remember, the offering isn't just in the Old Testament. In the New Testament (Mark 12:41-44; Luke 21:1-4), Jesus stood by the treasury in the Temple and watched what everyone contributed. When everyone finished giving, my version of his reply is, "Out of all you jokers that gave today, the only person that gave something that mattered was this woman. You all gave a tiny part of your excess, but she gave everything she had."

Everyone gave that day, but God didn't care about any of their gifts. You hear people say, "It's okay to give, even if you only give two pennies like the woman with two mites." No! No one in America or Canada only has two pennies to give. It's ridiculous to teach like that. Those two pennies were all she had. When she put everything that she had in the offering, it provoked God to action.

Brother Schambach tells of an A. A. Allen meeting where a boy was healed of 26 diseases at once. It was the mid 20th century. The boy was two years old. He was blind in both eyes, deaf in both ears, and unable to speak. No male parts had formed in his body and the bones in both of his legs were deformed. He received healed! It was an incredible miracle but most don't know the story of what transpired before the miracle occurred. The boy's mother had saved $20 to take the bus home after the meeting. That night, the Lord spoke to her to put the $20 in the offering, leaving her with no way to get home. It was a crusade with thousands, so Brother Allen had no clue who this woman was or what she had done. After she placed her money in the offering, Brother Allen said, "I see someone who traveled here from Tennessee by bus. You have a son with 26 diseases. Bring the boy up here." She brought her son up and he was healed!

But that was only the first part of the miracle. People were so thrilled by the healing that they began to give the woman an offering. People came and showered her with money. She left with several hundred dollars. It was a dual miracle provoked by a real offering of faith.

There is one offering I can pinpoint that turned everything around for me. It was before I was married. I went to a church in Virginia Beach, Virginia to hear Brother Schambach speak. At the last minute he was unable to attend and another well-known speaker filled in. He was known as a prosperity preacher. I had been taught in Bible College that prosperity was of the devil and ministers who taught prosperity were just trying to get your money. So initially, I was upset that he was the replacement speaker.

My body was physically whole, so I was open to hearing about healing. On the other hand, I was broke and didn't want to hear anything about prosperity. I knew these ministers were experts in taking offerings and I figured they knew how to manipulate people to give. I resolved that he wouldn't manipulate me, I'd leave my wallet under the front seat of my car. That way, even if he was a successful manipulator and I felt compelled to give, my wallet would be in my car. I could say, "Oops! Sorry Lord. The wallet is in my car. I really wanted to give but I don't want to disrupt the service."

The speaker went on to preach for an hour and a half. He used countless Scriptures, many that I'd never heard before. It's funny how people who don't believe in prosperity keep you blind to the massive amount of scriptures that talk about God financially and materially enriching His children. Even though I was off-track doctrinally at the time, I do hold the Word of God above all else. If you can show it to me in the Bible, then I will change my mind to line up with what the Bible says. I realized that night that prosperity is the will of God. Giving is a main highway to that prosperity.

When they received the offering that night, I felt the Lord strongly instruct me to give everything I had. I went out and got my wallet from under my seat. I took out my bankcard and filled out an offering envelope. At the time I didn't even know how much money I had in the bank. Back then I never looked at my account balance because it was too painful. The amount was always so low that I'd become depressed. I remembered that I had at least $72 dollars in the bank. I wrote an offering for $72 dollars and gave it all. I didn't have any money left in my checking account. I didn't have a savings account. All my money was gone. I had no credit cards for backup. I was BROKE. I wouldn't be getting paid for another ten days so I figured I'd just go on a 10-day fast. It's very easy to fast when you don't have money to get food. Even if you feel your stomach growl, you can't do anything about it, unless you rob a Burger King or Taco Bell.

I worked for a ministry at the time that gave me a standardized honorarium. I had a set salary. Even if a preaching opportunity opened up, the money went to the ministry. At the time, there was really no way for me to get any more money. When I turned around from the altar to walk back to my seat, a lady stopped me in the aisle. She said, "How can I give to you?" I replied, "Who, me? I don't have anything to do with this ministry that's here tonight." She said, "No, the Lord spoke to me to give to *you*." I started to give her the name of the ministry I worked for and she interrupted me saying, "No. God told me, 'Don't give to his ministry, give to him.'"

I had never heard that before in my life. People always told me the opposite, "Now this isn't for you, this is for the ministry." I followed up and asked the woman, "Are you sure? You realize you won't receive any IRS receipt for doing that? No tax credit." She said, "I don't want any tax credit. I want to be obedient to what the Lord told me." I conceded and gave her my name. She wrote the check and handed it to me. I folded it in half and put it in my Bible.

When I got back to my seat, I was very excited to see what amount was on the check. Whatever the amount, I'd be able to make it work. If it was for $10, I could at least get a Taco Bell value meal that night. Then I could wait three days and get another value meal, spacing it out until my next paycheck. I could live off that. I unfolded it and saw a check for $1,000. It was the first $1,000 check I'd ever received. The next morning I shamelessly went to the bank and cashed the check. I went from being completely broke to walking around with ten $100 bills in my wallet and the biggest smile on my face.

I recognized that when God spoke to me to give in the offering, He was not trying to take money *from me*. He was trying to get money *to me*. Before God will get the money to you, you have to give. **"Give, and you will receive. Your gift will return to you in full – pressed down, shaken together to make room for more, running over, and poured into your lap. The amount you give will determine the amount you get back"** (Luke 6:38).

Most people have never given an offering that moves God. Most preachers at a minister's conference will put less money in the offering that night, than they will on a restaurant afterwards. They have big bellies and small bank accounts. They put a priority on their life, food, and house, but they have never put that same priority on God's house. This is why they stay at a low level.

Since that meeting in Virginia Beach, I've found that when you put God first in your giving, it's a test. He doesn't need it. He has streets paved with gold and fences of jasper, onyx, and pearl. Does he need my $72 USD? No, God will never need my money. It's me who needs an open window of heaven over my life, which is activated by giving the tithe and the offering.

First Fruits Giving

"When you enter the land the LORD your God is giving you as a special possession and you have conquered it and settled there, put some of the first produce from each crop you harvest into a basket and bring it to the designated place of worship – the place the LORD your God chooses for his name to be honored. Go to the priest in charge at that time and say to him, 'With this gift I acknowledge to the LORD your God that I have entered the land he swore to our ancestors he would give us.' The priest will then take the basket from your hand and set it before the altar of the LORD your God. "You must then say in the presence of the LORD your God, 'My ancestor Jacob was a wandering Aramean who went to live as a foreigner in Egypt. His family arrived few in number, but in Egypt they became a large and mighty nation."

DEUTERONOMY 26:1-5

Several types of giving we're going to address are presented to different entities – such as to the church, to a ministry, and even to a man. It's a biblical principle to not only honor God but additionally, honor men of God. The first fruit offering is to be brought to the priest.

More often than not, first fruits giving is left out of the American church's teaching. If a minister taught on the principle, most would criticize and comment, "Look at this guy who prepared a whole sermon just to tell us that we're to honor him with gifts!" Multitudes will miss out on what the Bible says because ministers are afraid of what people will think of them. Whenever I preach at churches, I make it a point to preach on these principles. In doing so, I've found that pastors always thank me afterwards.

Ministers, don't worry what people will think because this is for their benefit, not your own. People need scriptural teaching. The first fruit offering can be brought to the priest or a minister – it's given to a man of God to bless them. So what exactly is a first fruits offering? As an example, let's say you make $3,000 a month at your job and receive a raise of $400 a month. The first month that you receive your check of $3,400, you take the extra $400 (that you haven't been living on) and bring it to a minister to show God that you know the increase is coming from Him. By acknowledging that the increase comes from God, you set yourself apart for further increase.

"Honor the Lord with your wealth and with the best part of everything you produce. Then he will fill your barns with grain, and your vats will overflow with good wine."

PROVERBS 3:9-10

You don't have to give $400 each month for the rest of your life – just give the money that first month. Instead of devouring it you say, "Father, I know I've been living on $3,000 a month but because of you I have this extra $400, so the first $400 goes back to you." First fruit is not for the church, it's for you to bless a minister. Bring your first fruit to a *real minister*, don't disguise it. Don't give it to your son who's in Bible College to help him pay his school loan. It's imperative to let go of seed. My wife and I don't tithe to our own ministry nor do our employees. We tithe to our church because that's where our tithe belongs. In the same respect, our ministry tithes to other ministries.

When you give your first fruit, God will see to it that it won't be the last time you receive a raise. From that point forward, you'll have plenty of first fruit offerings to bring because you're honoring God. You're showing God you understand that it's not your *own* hands bringing you wealth, it's *Him* bringing you into this land.

Almsgiving

"Whoever gives to the poor will lack nothing, but those who close their eyes to poverty will be cursed."

PROVERBS 28:27

In the *King James Version* of the Bible, giving to the poor is often referred to as *almsgiving*. Jesus refers to this type of giving in Matthew 6:3 when he says, **"But when you give to someone in need, don't let your left hand know what your right hand is doing."** It's not wrong to give in public as an example to others. David told the people what he was giving to the Lord in 1 Chronicles 29 and Barnabas gave the money from the sale of his land to the apostles in Acts 4. It's *giving to the poor* that the Bible instructs not to do publicly. He scolded the Pharisees and Sadducees for blowing trumpets in the street when they gave to the poor. When you give to the poor, do it discreetly to protect the dignity of the person you're helping. Don't have someone bring a video camera and record it for your YouTube channel. Instead, preserve the individual's dignity and help them quietly.

"Oh, the joys of those who are kind to the poor! The LORD rescues them when they are in trouble. The LORD protects them and keeps them alive. He gives them prosperity in the land and rescues them from their enemies. The LORD nurses them when they are sick and restores them to health."

PSALMS 41:1-3

When you give to the poor, the Lord...

1. Rescues you when you are in trouble
2. Protects you
3. Keeps you alive
4. Gives you prosperity in the land
5. Rescues you from your enemies
6. Nurses you when you are sick
7. Restores you to health

Giving to the poor changed my life. When I saw poverty for the first time in India, I called home to the United States and made a vow to feed 40 children a month overseas. I had never seen real poverty before and I felt the Lord instruct me to do something about it. Feeding 40 children a month was a big deal at that time, because it was equivalent to the monthly rent for our apartment. After I returned from India, we received close to $92,000 dollars in the offering at one church alone. Prior to, the largest amount the church had ever collected for a guest speaker was $5,000! This event proved to me that God takes care of those who give to the poor.

When we increased our giving to feed 80 children a month, the money continued to flow. Then in January 2015, we increased to feeding 200 children a month. Afterwards, we received $180,000 from a church where previously $5,500 was the largest amount given to a guest speaker. Our next increase was to 400 children, and currently we feed 800 children a day from our ministry.

The sevenfold blessing is powerful! It's an all-around, all-encompassing blessing for helping the poor. When I refer to helping the poor, I'm talking about a concerted giving effort. If you partner with our ministry, you're already doing that each month. A one-time gift of $5 to a homeless man on the street doesn't qualify for the sevenfold blessing. It requires a concerted effort to take your resources and help the destitute.

I encourage you to help those overseas. The poverty level is different in central Africa or India, where there's no access to food. As opposed to America, where oftentimes children are poor because their parents spend all their money on drugs. In America, you have access to resources. Overseas, there are children with access to nothing. God promised that if you do something about it, He will bless your life in every area.

Sacrificial Giving

What is an offering of sacrifice? An offering of sacrifice is not simply giving your best, it's giving *beyond* your best. Abraham is an example of a man who gave beyond his best. Abraham offering Isaac to the Lord as a sacrifice was not his best. His son was *beyond* his best. When God sent Jesus,

He wasn't giving His best. He was giving *beyond* His best. God gave His only Son to mankind to be slaughtered. Look at the harvest it produced! Today, sons and daughters are still being led into the kingdom of God.

Oftentimes, an offering of sacrifice is when God asks you to give everything. In my twenties, I cleared out my bank account two different times and gave everything to the Lord. If you're sensitive to the voice of the Lord, there will be a time in your Christianity where God will ask you to give an offering of sacrifice. When the Lord lays it on your heart, you won't be able to deny the feeling.

In December 2015, I went to Nigeria to attend Bishop Oyedepo's Shiloh Conference. At the conference they received an offering of sacrifice that the people had been preparing for all year. They were instructed to give an offering that truly represented something of value. While I was standing there, I saw people with tears in their eyes, lifting their envelopes to God. You could tell that not only were they giving their best, but *beyond* their best.

As I stood there, I hated that I didn't have anything to give. I had things back home in the U.S., but nothing I could access. You can only withdrawal a few nairas from the ATM and the conversion rate is 312 naira to $1 USD. The most I could withdrawal was around $80 USD. No credit card companies do business in Nigeria because there's so much bank fraud – so that wasn't an option. Moreover, I couldn't stand there in good conscience, holding up $80 dollars as if it was a massive offering that brought tears to my eyes.

As I was thinking about how terrible I felt, I glanced down at my left wrist and saw the Rolex watch someone had given me. I've always liked watches and it was the most valuable personal possession I owned. The last time I checked it was worth $14,100. As soon as my eyes locked on that watch, I knew it was the sacrifice I was supposed to give that day. When I saw Bishop Oyedepo later that day, I put it in his hand and said, "This is from me to you, Merry Christmas." I was giving it to him as a sacrifice. It hurt, believe me, I felt it. I gave away the most valuable thing I owned. Just over a month later, someone gave me a limited edition Breitling watch. Only 2,000 of that kind had been crafted and it's worth more than the watch I gave away. I know that return was triggered by my sacrifice.

I'm not suggesting that giving my watch away is equal to Abraham sacrificing Isaac or God sacrificing Jesus. At the time, it was the most valuable thing I had to give. I liked that watch, it meant something to me. When the Lord put His finger on it, I gave it. Furthermore, it triggered the most abundant year we've had in the history of our ministry. Sacrifice is not giving your best, it's giving *beyond* your best.

In Matthew 26, the woman with the alabaster jar gave sacrificially. The jar she broke was valued at more than a year's worth of wages. She was crying as she offered it to Jesus. If there are no tears in your eyes when you give, it's not an offering of sacrifice. I would challenge you not to let your life end without giving an offering that brings tears to your eyes. **"Wherever your treasure is, there the desires of your heart will also be"** (Matthew 6:21).

Honoring a Man of God

"[The wealthy woman] said to her husband, 'I am sure this man who stops in from time to time is a holy man of God. Let's build a small room for him on the roof and furnish it with a bed, a table, a chair, and a lamp. Then he will have a place to stay whenever he comes by.'"

2 KINGS 4:9-10

The Shunammite woman and her husband built and furnished a room for Elisha. It had a private entrance and exit so that when Elisha came by, he'd have a place to rest and study. When the Shunammite woman honored Elisha as a man of God, his heart was set to bless her. Elisha told his servant to ask her what she needed. Even though the Shunammite woman told them she didn't need anything, Elisha's servant noticed she didn't have any children. Elisha called her back and said, **"... Next year at this time you will be holding a son in your arms"** (2 Kings 4:16). Sure enough, she was holding a son by that time the following year.

Honoring a man of God triggered a blessing that money can't buy. When you make it your business to bless men of God, God will see to it that He blesses you. When Brother Kenneth Hagin was alive, there was a minister that made it a point to give him a large offering each time he saw him. Within 30 days, the minister would always see a major return come back to his hand.

Honoring a man of God is a concept that's been lost in America. The Bible teaches to honor men of God. I've made it a point to be my pastor's greatest source of blessing. If I find out someone did something nice for him, I make it a point to do something nicer. Selfishly, I know that if I honor men of God, God will honor me.

Dr. Rodney Howard-Browne shares the following story about me publicly; otherwise I wouldn't personally share it. One time I found out where he was preaching and booked him and his wife the nicest hotel in that city for the week. He said that in all his years of ministry, no one had ever done that before. I did that to honor a man of God. In doing so, God has always honored me. What you make happen for others, God makes happen for you.

Many people in America neglect the principle of honoring a man of God. On pastor appreciation day, churches with 500 people will give their pastor a collective $100 gift card to Applebee's. That irritates God! One time as I was leaving the parking lot after preaching at a church, I noticed the pastor having trouble starting his car. I thought I'd have to give him a ride home and call a tow truck. He finally got the old, beat-up car to turn over. Everyone else had left and I was the only one that waited to see if his car would start. I felt the Lord speak to me, "That is why these people aren't blessed." Even though I was trying my best to minister at the church, I hadn't seen any kind of breakthrough. It was as if God had no interest in the church having revival. God said, "Until they learn to honor their pastor, I will never honor them." God takes who you honor seriously. You should treat the minister that God's placed in your life, as you would treat Jesus.

"And the King will say, 'I tell you the truth, when you did it to one of the least of these my brothers and sisters, you were doing it to me!'"

MATTHEW 25:40

Let me offer an encouraging example of honoring a man of God. I used to stay in people's homes when I went to preach. The first time I ever preached in Montreal, Canada, I stayed with a couple and their two children. The wife's name was Angie. She treated me as if I was a foreign dignitary. I couldn't receive better treatment at the White House! She was Italian and made five-course breakfasts each morning and five-course dinners every night. I would preach a youth meeting, go out afterwards with the youth group, and not return until one or two in the morning. Upon my return I expected to just crash in bed, but Angie would have a massive meal waiting. She bought me a suit, shirt, and tie. I told her that I'd never received such hospitable treatment before. She replied, "The Bible says that you're to receive ministers as if they are Jesus, so I'm treating you as I would treat Jesus if He was in my home." Her answer and generosity blew me away!

Even if your pastor is not a world-changing, planet-shaking minister, God said whatever you've done unto the least of these, you've done to me. Honor them as if you're honoring Jesus; and the return doesn't come from your pastor, the return comes from God.

Partner with a Traveling Ministry

People think Jesus operated magically on the earth but He didn't. Do you ever wonder how Jesus paid his bills?

"Soon afterward Jesus began a tour of the nearby towns and villages, preaching and announcing the Good News about the Kingdom of God. He took his twelve disciples with him, along with some women who had been cured of evil spirits and diseases. Among them were Mary Magdalene, from whom he had cast out seven demons; Joanna, the wife of Chuza, Herod's business manager; Susanna; and many others who were contributing from their own resources to support Jesus and his disciples."

LUKE 8:1-3

Jesus was on a preaching tour. There were women that made it their business to finance Jesus by continuing to contribute from their own personal resources. In Philippians 4, Paul talks about how the Philippian church was the only one partnering with his ministry financially. Because of this, Paul stated that the Philippian church were partakers of the grace that was on his ministry. The Philippian church made it their business to send financial gifts Paul's way as he traveled. The same God that supplied all of Paul's needs would supply all of their needs according to his riches in glory.

Comparably, the Shunammite woman was a partaker of the grace of Elisha, as he was a travelling minister. She made it her business to make sure Elisha was cared for.

First, she made sure he had food. Second, she made sure he had a place to stay. It released the following four blessings on her behalf:

1. God gave her a son. What money couldn't buy was given to her.
2. When the son died, Elisha made it his personal business to rebuke death and bring her son back to life.
3. Elisha gave the woman a notice about a famine that was coming to the land.
4. After the famine was over, God divinely used Elisha and his servant to restore the woman's property to her, along with the value of all the crops harvested in her absence.

Partnering with a travelling ministry puts an end to all losses personally and in business according to the Word of God (2 Kings 4; Philippians 4:11-19). God ensures you're privileged to divine instruction so that you never go backwards – He leads you forward.

"Thus says the LORD, your Redeemer, the Holy One of Israel: 'I am the LORD your God, Who teaches you to profit, Who leads you by the way you should go.'"

ISAIAH 48:17, NKJV

God wants to prosper you so that you're able to support and partner with ministries. If there's an economic downturn coming, God will give you notice so you can stay ahead of it. From this day forward, God is going to open the windows of Heaven over your life, even from a young age. I hope there are 16, 17, and 18 years olds reading this book. I'm sure people are already trying to convince you about the importance of good credit. Advising you to get a credit card, in order to build good credit, and get approved for loans. No, the Bible says you will lend to many and never borrow from anyone. If you apply these principles, you'll easily pay cash for everything you do. Just like Adalis and I do in our lives and in our ministry. That's the blessing that's coming upon your life today, in Jesus' name.

Chapter 7

Divine Leading

*"... I am the LORD your God, who teaches you to profit,
who leads you by the way you should go."*

ISAIAH 48:17, NKJV

When God brought us from a negative bank balance to a million dollar account, He did it during a breakthrough time. Of course like anything with God, the breakthrough never stopped – it just continued. Breakthrough is not an accident. Breakthrough is not something you wait for to happen. The degree to which you engage the Word of God and it's principles will produce your level of breakthrough.

God's Word is for our profiting. As soon as that clicks in your spirit, it becomes very easy to search out and obey God's commands. You realize they're not just commands so you can be a Christian or make heaven, but they'll truly cause you to prosper and break forth in every area of life. When you recognize that God rendered those commands not for His benefit but yours, it becomes a delight to keep the commands of God.

God never leads backwards. God never leads into stagnation. God promised that if you follow Him, He'll lead you forward into abundance. Choose to be led by the Spirit. As Romans 8:14 states, **"For all who are led by the Spirit of God are children of God."**

Jesus said my sheep know my voice (John 10:27). Once you are born again, you have access to the frequency on which God broadcasts. It's not a matter of *if* a Christian can be led by the Spirit. It's a matter of *taking the time* to be led by the Spirit. That's why the baptism of the Holy Ghost and praying in tongues is imperative. 1 Corinthians 14:2 says,

"For if you have the ability to speak in tongues, you will be talking only to God, since people won't be able to understand you. You will be speaking by the power of the Spirit, but it will all be mysterious."

1 CORINTHIANS 14:2

When you speak in your prayer language, it's unprofitable for the people around you since they don't understand the language. When you pray in the Spirit, you're making a connection with the Spirit of God and tuning into that frequency. When you're led by God's Spirit, you'll always be led into profiting. If you're led by your own good ideas, what others think, or whatever else you substitute for the leading of God, it becomes easy to make bad moves.

You cannot go to the top without divine leading. Human wisdom will only get you so far. There's a wisdom that's higher than all wisdom, and that wisdom comes from divine leading.

Scripturally, there are four sources of wisdom:

There is **sensual wisdom,** which is common wisdom you inherit as a human being. For example, when a baby is born it doesn't take its mother's nipple and put it in its ear. Without having to go to any type of breastfeeding school, babies instinctually know to put the breast in their mouth to get food. Sensual wisdom is what most people have from their animal nature.

There is **acquired wisdom**, which is the type of wisdom you receive through higher education. This wisdom isn't as profitable as a lot of people think. These days you'll find numerous people with Master's degrees to which they've only practiced the ability to get a nose ring and pour coffee.

Devilish "wisdom" is a demonic wisdom that witch doctors, psychics, and other demonized people have access to. However, the devil doesn't know what's going to happen five seconds from now, so to a degree it's in the supernatural realm of knowledge.

God's wisdom is above all. God's wisdom is the highest of all wisdom. Job 28 refers to this type of wisdom and describes that not even the sea or earth know anything about it because it's in the Heavens with God. When you access God's wisdom, it lifts you above all wisdoms this earth could ever offer. This is the wisdom that can set you on high above all the nations of the world (Deuteronomy 28:1).

In Genesis 12, God tells Abraham to leave his country and father's home and go to the land He would show him. God promised that He would bless Abraham and make him a blessing – that through him all the nations of the earth would be blessed. Everything Abraham accomplished and was rewarded for, started with a divine leading. Make allowances for the same divine leading in your life. If you have no prayer life, spend no time with God, and have no leading from God, you're not going to enjoy supernatural abundance.

"Thus says the LORD to His anointed, to Cyrus, whose right hand I have held, to subdue nations before him and loose the armor of kings, to open before him the double doors, so that the gates will not be shut. 'I will go before you and make the crooked places straight; I will break in pieces the gates of bronze and cut the bars of iron.'"

ISAIAH 45:1-2, NKJV

When God leads you, He goes before you and knocks every obstacle out of your way. That's the difference between people that do things by divine leading and people that do things by good ideas. There's an effortless triumph with people that are led by the Spirit, because God goes before them and deals with all possible challenges.

You ought to be able to know that God sent you. I know God sent me to be an evangelist to the United States. It gives me confidence to acknowledge that whatsoever may be an obstacle or an enemy, is not my enemy. They're God's enemy because I'm not out there doing my own thing. I didn't decide to be in this line of work because I like public speaking, wanted to buy some fancy suits, or simply talk about the Bible – I was sent by God. God led me to what I do today.

"I will give you the treasures of darkness and hidden riches of secret places, that you may know that I, the LORD, who call you by your name, Am the God of Israel."

ISAIAH 45:3, NKJV

God will go before you and make the crooked places straight, cut down the gates of iron, and smash down everything that's in your way. On top of that, He'll lead you to the hidden treasures, the riches of secret places, the treasures of darkness, and the wealth of the wicked. By His wisdom, God will show you a way to receive those things through divine leading.

Develop a routine where you spend time with God. Like a radio show, God has a frequency He broadcasts on. If you never tune into the show, you'll never hear what He's saying. You don't have to beg God to speak, He's always speaking, but it's your responsibility to dial into the frequency. In the same way that you can't rewind a radio program, you can't go back to when God tried to speak to you and find out what you've missed. If you missed it, you missed it. This exhibits the importance of prayer. God is speaking pertinent information every day. If you spend time with Him, He'll clue you in on His wisdom. His wisdom will help take care of any obstacles in your way and give you the treasures of darkness and riches in secret places.

I know a couple that were getting ready to buy a house and property. The Lord spoke to the wife in prayer and said,

"The property that you looked at yesterday, there's treasure on that land." She told her husband, he listened to her, and they bought the property. She had her youngest son use a metal detector to look for treasure over all the acres. He found nothing. Time went by and they thought, "Well, she thought she heard from God, but I guess she didn't."

Decades later, they discovered that their property was on top of natural gas wells. They not only found one natural gas well, they found multiple gas wells on that property. The company paid them $250,000 for the rights to drill and obtain the gas, and an additional $10,000 per well, per month. It brought them into riches. That is millions and millions of dollars that's going to be passed down through their family. The family received a generational blessing by obeying one instruction from God.

You need to have a divine encounter with God where you find out His will for your life. Two years ago I was speaking at a church on divine leading. I told the church the story of how an angel appeared in my room when I was young and told me I was to be an evangelist. I said to the crowd, "Now most people are not going to have an encounter like that. Most people are just going to read the principles of God's Word and then know what they're to do for their life." I immediately felt convicted after those words came out of my mouth. After the meeting, I felt the Lord speak to my spirit, "You know very clearly that my Word says in Acts 10, that God is no respecter of persons. It's not like I just did that for you because you're special and I won't do it for other people. What drew an angel to come and tell you what to do with your life, is that you were seeking after me and had a desire in your heart for my kingdom – and so I led you. And I will do that for anyone with the same desires."

Prophets of God throughout the Bible such as Gideon, Moses, Abraham, Isaac, Jacob, Jonah, and Paul – all had dramatic encounters with God, an angel, or some sort of vision. They each experienced something that shook them to the core, along with clear instructions. I'm not saying you should lock yourself in a room and demand God visit you. You don't seek after the supernatural in such a way because that's how one can be deceived. If you strive to hear a voice, the devil will accommodate you and you'll start hearing voices. Most people wouldn't be spiritually mature or intelligent enough to discern whether it was God or the devil. Spend time with God and allow His grace to create a desire in your spirit to make an impact for the kingdom of God. When you do that, you'll have an encounter with the voice of God, dreams, visions, or something similar.

"In the last days, God says, I will pour out my Spirit upon all people. Your sons and daughters will prophesy. Your young men will see visions, and your old men will dream dreams."

ACTS 2:17

Acts 2:17 is a promise from God. If you've lived your whole life without any kind of supernatural leading, you ought to either check the time you're spending with God or your desire. Check if you have an American spirit that only wants to pay the bills and have a nice house or whether you truly have a desire to build the kingdom of God.

Before the angel appeared to me at seven years old, I used to stand on the street corner of our housing development with a poster that read, "Jesus loves you." I was preaching and recording sermons on my Mr. Potato Head tape recorder at 3 years old. By listening to my dad's sermons on heaven, hell, and Bible prophecy, I developed the desire in my spirit for people to be saved. It was the most important thing in my life and it attracted a supernatural encounter with God. It was the opportunity for God to say, "Okay, I've got something for you to do. I'm going to tell you how to do it."

First and foremost, one must have a desire for the advancement of God's kingdom. After obtaining that desire, be open to having a divine encounter. Spend time in fasting and prayer. It sets you apart to know God and have Him visit you. You can't think of a divine encounter, vision, dream, or angel visitation as something for only a select few. Study the Bible and you'll find that anyone who set themselves apart to be used by God, had an encounter with God. Your case won't be any different because God is not a respecter of persons (Acts 10:34).

Your Breakthrough is Tied to a Place

"... The LORD is my shepherd, I lack nothing."

Psalms 23:1, NIV

Allow God to lead in every aspect of your life. Additionally, you must understand that your breakthrough

110

is tied to a place. Jonah was a prophet so mightily anointed that his ministry caused the entire city of Nineveh to go on a 40-day fast. The Bible says in Jonah 3 that even the animals ate nothing. That's a powerful anointing! The Lord told him to go to Nineveh but Jonah disobeyed His command and set off on a ship away from Nineveh. When Jonah was headed in the wrong direction, he became cursed. He was so cursed that the heathen people on the boat noticed. They pulled Jonah aside and said, "Brother, you have a problem. Ever since you got on this boat, things have been going wrong. We've traced it to you. We need you off this boat."

Jonah's dismal state demonstrates the truth that a person can never become so anointed that they outgrow divine direction. A person ought to be continually gaining instruction from God. There are ministers who received an instruction from God in 1995 and have been repeating it for years. They never receive any kind of fresh word or update of what God wants them to do, they become stagnant. Be led as to what God has for you to do. Then seek to regularly hear His voice in order to receive updated, pertinent, specific instruction.

You can't live anywhere you want. The majority of people live near their parents, where their mother wants them to live. I'm not talking about teenagers; I'm talking about 56 year olds that live where they grew up. They proclaim, "I need to be close to my mother because if I wasn't here, there would be no one to visit her." They don't make any decisions based on God's leading.

I become extremely concerned when I listen to people talk about where they live and I don't hear, "I heard the Lord say..." It's always, "Well, my wife likes the Columbus, Ohio area. We've always felt this area needed a church." I listen to them, all the while, with a feeling that they're going to struggle in life. If the reason you started a church, went into the ministry, or started your business was because you felt like it would be a good idea – you need to have an encounter with the Lord. You need to hear the Lord give you direction. If you're going in the wrong direction like Jonah, it doesn't matter how much anointing you carry. If you're called to Nineveh and you're going away from Nineveh, you're cursed.

There's a pastor that went to Bible school with my father. He felt his time was up at the church he was pastoring, so he asked the Lord to open up a big ministry opportunity. Sure enough, he received telephone calls from three large churches. He pastored a church of less than 200 people, whereas these churches sat approximately 700 to 1,100 people. Any one of these opportunities would be a major level change and answer to his prayer. After visiting one church in particular, he felt led in his spirit that it was the one to pastor. A few months later, I noticed that he hadn't moved and asked, "Why haven't you gone?" He said, "Oh, my wife said that we would live too far away from her mother, and we need to be close enough to visit." You can't put a restriction like that on God.

He might as well of prayed, "God I'll go anywhere you want me to go. I'll do anything you want me to do. I'll say anything you want me to say. As long as it's within a 50 mile radius of where my mother-in-law lives." You can't live like that. You have to make yourself the Lord's servant, willing to go and do whatever He says. Think about how many people are called into Bible school and allow someone to discourage them from going. They'll quip, "Florida is quite a long ways to go. I don't know if that's wise at your age. You're only an 18 year old girl." People allow others to talk them out of what God has called them to do. Their life from that point forward is stagnant because they missed the opportunity God prepared for them.

If God gives you an instruction and you refuse to obey, you'll spend the rest of your life out of the will of God. God doesn't then create a second will for your life based on your disobedience. Every person you meet is someone God never intended for you to meet. Why do you think most people marry a buffoon who ruins their life? It's because they didn't align their spirits for divine leading. You have to obey the voice of God.

Countless people don't experience a divine encounter with God because the Lord knows they won't listen even if He spoke to them. Don't let that be you! When God told Abraham, "Leave your father's family, leave your country, and go to the land that I will show you;" He didn't tell Abraham what land to go to, He just told Abraham to leave (Genesis 12:1). Abraham departed that same day. If you want Abraham's blessing, you have to live like Abraham did. Abraham didn't depart 15 years later, he departed immediately. Most people are too slow in obeying God's instructions. God will speak to them and they take an eternity to move on the instruction. Abraham's father Terah was an idol maker. There are times when God will have a person break free from their family to go somewhere else. Jesus wasn't honored in his own hometown. Oftentimes, you have to leave where you grew up to find the place where your breakthrough is tied.

God instructed Elijah to go sit and camp at Kerith. He told Elijah that ravens would feed him and that he could drink from the brook. Ravens didn't just follow Elijah anywhere; they followed him to the place where God had led him. When the brook dried up, God gave him a second instruction. Go to the village Zarephath, and you will find a widow gathering sticks. I've already given her my instruction to feed you (1 Kings 17:9). Elijah took God's divine leading seriously.

I once went to a minister's meeting that Bishop Oyedepo held in New York City. There were approximately 80 ministers in attendance. It was awesome to be in such a small setting with one of God's great servants. Bishop Oyedepo spent the whole time talking about Jonah. He told the pastors from Africa, "Many of you need to go back to Africa because God never called you to America. You just wanted to leave the problems of Africa and come to the United States so your kids can go to a better school. It doesn't work that way. You can't just decide you're sick of Africa and go to America. Then, because you're called into the ministry, you start a church in America. That's why many of you can't break 35 people on a Sunday morning. God never sent you here. You need to go back to Africa. There's a man here – you've traded a throne in Kenya for a folding chair in America."

What did Bishop Oyedepo mean by that? He maintained that God had those men in Africa to shake *that* nation. Instead, because they wanted to live in America, they have small struggling churches that will never make an impact because they're in the wrong place. Don't neglect the fact that your breakthrough is tied to a place.

Take your life seriously. Don't live where you want, live where God leads. Don't go to college anywhere, ask God where you should go. The majority of people choose to not consult God on anything. Make it a priority to consult God on *everything*. Pray in the morning. Ask God every day, "Lord, open my eyes. Let my spirit be sensitive to your voice. Lead me today, in Jesus' name."

Pray this prayer: *Father, let us never miss your voice. Let us hear your voice saying, "This is the way, walk ye therein." Let us have a grace where we, like Abraham, never wait more than 24 hours to obey whatever you've told us to do. Let us be people that move quickly, that follow the pillar of cloud and the pillar of fire. Let us be sensitive to your voice. Let us not only hear your voice, but also obey your voice. Give us a grace to pray without ceasing, to spend our mornings in prayer, and to set apart times throughout the day to seek your face. Let us be sensitive to your voice so we don't choose to live like the people around us in our culture and throughout the world – blown by the wind, led by their problems and their own carnal thinking. Let us be people that are led by your Spirit, for you said in Romans 8:14, that as many who are led by the Spirit of God, they are the sons and daughters of God. We thank and give you praise that since we're your children, we can hear your voice. We don't have to get our information from the news. We can hear your voice, and in hearing your voice, we can have access to your leading – which will always lead away from trouble and into profiting. Let there be a change in my life to that effect, from this day forward, in Jesus' mighty name.*

CHAPTER 8

The Power of Wise Planning

"Any enterprise is built by wise planning, becomes strong through common sense, and profits wonderfully by keeping abreast of the facts."

PROVERBS 24:3-4, TLB

Believing God is not a plan. If you leave everything in that realm of thinking, you're going to be poor.

"How is your church going to grow this year, Pastor?"

"Well, we just believe God is going to send people in!"

"How is your business doing?"

"It's not doing good right now, but I'm believing God that our business is going to increase."

"How do you believe your business is going to increase?"

"I just believe that the Lord will make a way where there is no way."

Most people who grew up Pentecostal know that they're unwise planners. Everything is left in the ethereal realm, waiting for angels to do what God told them to do. Proverbs 24 says that a house is built by wisdom, wise planning, and knowledge. The good news is that you don't have to choose between being spiritual and being a wise planner.

Life is not mystical.

Life is practical.

Think about the poor places of the world. They're the places that practice witchcraft and have no structure, leaving the ethereal realm to govern their country. Now think about the prosperous places of the world. Their governments have concrete plans and they take action to accomplish goals and establish stability.

Do you know why there are so many poor Christian businesses and rich secular businesses? If a Christian has a business and their finances are drying up, most of them view it as an attack of the devil. They will fast, pray, and read books on the gifts of the Spirit to rectify the problem. On the other hand, if a sinner's revenue source begins to dry up, they don't see it as an attack of the devil. They don't defer to God to help them. They use their common sense to uncover the cause of the problem and develop a plan of action to defeat it.

Some Christians blame everything on the devil and ask the Lord to come through on their behalf. Don't misunderstand what I'm saying, the supernatural is real. The Holy Spirit will anoint your mind to make plans that are supernatural and give you quality meditative thoughts that address any problems. It's not a choice between believing in the supernatural and being a wise planner.

Let's use the Prodigal Son as an example. His story can be found in Luke 15:11-32. Think about how everything turned around for him. He spent every last penny and was out of money. He was sitting with the pigs, eating pig slop. Subsequently, everything changed through quality thinking and planning. Verse 17 says, **"When he finally came to his senses..."** All he needed to do was sit and think. To paraphrase his thought process – "My father will never take me back as a son after the way I treated and disgraced him. However, I know he needs servants. If I go back now, he'll hire me as a servant, and I'll be living better than I am today." He made a plan and everything turned around for him. Let's break down what wise planning entails.

God Will Not Work it Out Alone

God has done everything He's going to do. He sent Jesus – Jesus accomplished His work and ascended into Heaven. The Holy Spirit has been sent. The Word of God is available to you; all power has been given unto you. It's not God who's going to take care of your problems, it's you who has to develop a plan to address them. God won't do the legwork for you, you must work things out.

Dr. Benson Idahosa once said, "God gave you a brain so you could give Him a break." God gave you a brain so you wouldn't have to be a helpless human being, throwing yourself on the floor every day and crying out to God – "I need help!", "I need bread!", "I need water!", "I need clothes!"

1 Corinthians 2:16 says that we have the mind of Christ. Say that to yourself, "*I have the mind of Christ.*" Perhaps you were told that you were dumb in school or considered by others unintelligent. When you got saved and were born again, redeemed by the blood of Jesus – your old life died. All things are new, and God gave you a mind to work out every problem.

When we were doing a crusade in Philadelphia, Pennsylvania, our permit was initially revoked. I was discouraged when I heard the news but the Holy Spirit encouraged me in a very odd way – the mafia. I've not only watched most mafia movies, but I've read just about everything there is on the history of the Italian mafia in the United States. The mafia, with carnal minds destroyed by cocaine, alcohol, and disease had the ability to outthink the government. I said to myself, "How much more capable am I, filled with the Holy Spirit and operating with the mind of Christ, able to come up with a plan to defeat this government entity that's attempting to shut down the Crusade?" That thought process gave me confidence.

You don't just have a mind – you have the *mind of Christ*. Philippians 2:5 (NKJV) says, **"Let this mind be in you which was also in Christ Jesus."** With the mind of Christ, there's no obstacle that you can't defeat. When obstacles come up, you don't have to wait for God to do something about it. You also don't leave it solely in the realm of prayer. When you're praying, don't say, "Lord, I don't know what I'm going to do. I just leave this in your hands." No, to pray effectively say, "Lord, I know there's a way out. Show it to me in Jesus' name."

When I was preaching in the Caribbean, I offered bible college scholarships to everyone that felt a call to ministry. I spent one whole service preaching on the need for ministers – how the harvest is great and the laborers are few. I gave an altar call for anyone who wanted to give his or her life to Jesus Christ for full-time Christian service. For those saying, "No turning back, I'm giving everything. I won't stop for anything."

Twelve hours later, I received a direct message on Facebook from a young person who had received a full scholarship and would be able to attend Bible College tuition-free. All he had to do was get to Florida, which isn't far from the Caribbean. He told me that when he went to apply, there was a $50 application fee. The fee could only be processed using a credit card. He said that he couldn't go to Bible College because he didn't have a credit card. Unfortunately, if that's all it takes to stop you in life, you're going to do nothing.

A man in that position should plan to get a credit card. Think of all the options: borrow a family member's credit card, borrow a friend's credit card, or get your own credit card. Anyone can get a credit card, it's not that hard. They'll practically give them to pets at this point.

Similar to how the young man reacted is what most people do; they hit one challenge and wilt. Instead, when you hit a challenge say, "This is something in my way. How can I move this mountain? How can I go around it? How can I tunnel through it?" Any time something comes to stymie your progress, thank God that you have an anointed mind and use it to think your way out – like the Prodigal Son.

You Must Have Income

"How are you living?"
"Well, I'm living by faith!"

Many people believe this way, as if faith is a synonym for not working and doing nothing that produces money. It's essential that you have a source of income. It may sound obvious, but you'd be shocked by how many people don't realize you must have a source of income!

If you're not doing anything to produce income, you're living outside the will of God. The Bible instructs you to work. When it says *work*, it means *productive work* that produces resources to take care of yourself and your family. You should bear your own burden and never become a burden to others. Did you know that's a Biblical command? Galatians 6:5 (NKJV) states, **"For each one shall bear his own load."** In other words, your need for food is something God has empowered *you* to take care of. Not something you're believing God to have someone else take care of *for you*. You have to do something that generates income.

When God called Abraham, He told him that He would make him a great nation. Immediately, Abraham began ranching cattle, a practical action that produced income. Abraham didn't just rest in knowing that God had blessed him, that His Word was true, and that He would make a way where there seemed to be no way. He followed through with a practical action to produce income.

Living by faith is not living by poverty. Living by faith is not expecting other people to meet your needs. Living by faith is receiving financial empowerment from God to make you a blessing to others.

If you don't have income, you're disqualified from everything in this book. You need to work and have faith for a job that will provide adequate funds.

When I was in Bible College no one really had money. None of us students had any money, we were just, "poor Bible college students." I understood that I needed money to make car payments, pay for car insurance, college tuition, and food. I needed money to live.

When it came time for me to get a job, at first I thought I'd ask someone to help me get a job where they worked. Then it dawned on me, all of my working college friends were broke at their jobs. Rather than work the same jobs, I searched online for jobs that paid $20 per hour. A call center job came up in my search. I took the initiative and applied, simply doing what was required, and I got the job! I had an excess of spending money while I was in Bible College. Not by magic, but by work. Don't be a Bible college student that's depending on other people and hoping someone "blesses" you with money.

I want you to understand that God doesn't want you looking for people to *bless you*. God wants to make *you* the person that's blessing people. Don't get me wrong, God will send people in your path to bless you, but that shouldn't be the source of your income. You shouldn't be dependent on that source to pay your bills. People shouldn't have to hand you a sympathetic $100 because they can tell by the sad look on your face that things aren't going well, and you haven't eaten lately. That's no way to live! That's not how God wants you to live.

Make a plan that generates income. If you're in the ministry and hiding the fact that you don't have income, the Bible addresses your state. The Bible says that the laborer is worthy of his wages (Luke 10:7). When this verse is restated in 1 Timothy 5:18, it's prefaced in verse 17 with, **"Let the elders who rule well be counted worthy of double honor..."** Those who preach and teach the Word of God should be operating at double the standard of living, compared to where they're ministering.

Many people have it in their head that people should do ministry for free and consequently, don't pay them anything for their labor. A person shouldn't so extensively be working in ministry for free, that they're unable to get a job and therefore, have no money. Don't misunderstand this in relation to being involved in your church, there's nothing wrong with that. What's wrong is when people expect you to do ministry for 30 to 50 hours a week, for no pay, to the point where you can't work another job. There are married Bible college students doing this, not realizing that among other things, this puts a bad taste of the church in their children's mouths. Their children are not going to want to serve the Lord.

If children see their parents living poorly and never having enough, they're not going to believe the Bible when it says that God is a provider. If they see their parents serving Him diligently, yet continually lacking for everything, it just won't make sense. It's not right for someone to ask you to spend that amount of time in ministry for no pay. James 5:4 talks about laborers who have been denied their wages. When their cries reached the ears of the Lord, God saw it as wicked and brought condemnation. God wants people to be paid.

Everyone who works in our ministry is paid well. We don't tell our employees to just live by faith. Living by faith isn't some religious language you use to ask people to do without. The person in charge should not only have faith for themselves, but the faith to also provide for those with them. The Bible says faith is a tiny mustard seed that, when planted, becomes a mighty tree that birds make their nest in (Matthew 13:31-32).

If you're reading this as a Bible college student, you need to purge the mindset of living by faith without income, or undertaking full-time ministry for free. If you never have money and are always looking for someone to bless you, you'll function with the same mode of operation in the ministry. You won't have any money in the ministry and will continually seek out someone in the church with money – to bless or give you a place to stay.

During the infancy of my father's ministry, churches typically didn't take offerings for guest speakers. The church board would decide on an honorarium to give the guest speaker, which would typically be around $200 per week. It would barely cover my father's expenses to travel to his next engagement. In his first year of ministry, his total income was less than $5,600.

One day my father was praying for God to give him a plan. At the time, he had accumulated a little over $400 in the bank, more than he ever had before. God told him to take that money and buy a cassette duplicator to record his sermons and sell them at his table when he traveled. The purchase was $400, exhausting his money.

My dad wondered who in the world would want to buy his sermons. He didn't think he was a good preacher. Afterwards, at the first place he went, he sold a week's worth of sermons for a fairly small amount. He was in a mid-sized church that offered him a $200 honorarium and he sold over $600 worth of sermons. Shortly after that, my father preached a three-week revival. The honorarium was $1,500 and the tape sales were over $5,000. This plan that God gave my father was one of the first things that broke him and his ministry out of poverty.

God has a plan. God does make a way where there is no way. The way He makes for you is by giving you a way to get out. You won't find a passage in the Bible where God says, "Leave everything to me while you just sit there. I'm going to get you out." Even in 2 Chronicles 20:15 when God said, the battle is not yours, but God's, there was a plan. They had to go to Ziz and shout for the victory. The moment they began to sing and give praise to God, the Lord sent ambushes against their enemy and delivered them. You always have a role to play. Until you play your part, God won't play His.

Have a Budget

"... A fool spends whatever they get."

PROVERBS 21:20

What is a budget? It's essential to identify what income you have coming in. You have to know what expenses are going out. You need to document it. You should know what bills you have. If your bills exceed what's coming in, you're going to have a rough life.

If you have $1,200 coming in each month and $1,400 in bills, why not immediately cut out $500? Then you'll have $1,200 coming in each month and $900 in bills. Don't buy things by faith. You don't get an apartment by faith. You have to make a plan. Otherwise, you'll never enter into excess.

What's going out can't even be close to what's coming in. If you have $1,200 coming in, you cannot make a budget where your bills are $1,100. You have to factor in possibilities of repairs, car registrations, and replacing broken items. If you live on 100% of what comes in, you're always going to have a troubled and problematic life.

Plan for Increase

Increase is impossible without planning. Develop a financial plan on how to get from where you are now, to where God wants you to be. Have a plan of increase. Bishop David Oyedepo once said that the monthly overhead of your business should never exceed 30% of your revenue. Most evangelists I've been around usually exceed that percentage or spend all they have. One evangelist, who is very well-known, would run crusades in this way. If a crusade was going to cost $300,000, he'd get a 90 day loan for $300,000. He would then believe God to raise the $300,000 during the 90 days. At the end of the crusade, he and his staff would celebrate the fact that they were able to pay off the loan – as if it was a miracle.

If that's your mode of operation, you'll die with zero dollars in the bank. Your financial burden is passed down to your successor. When most ministers die, their funeral is used as a way to raise money or as an offering for seed in remembrance of the person. They don't leave any inheritance to their children or money to the ministry. They lived their entire lives week-to-week, paycheck-to-paycheck, and offering-to-offering.

Until I heard Bishop Oyedepo share on how his ministry operates, I believed that you were supposed to be spending everything that comes into the ministry. I learned that if God blesses you with more, you'll find more ways to spend it and expand the ministry. A fool spends whatever they get. God will fill your storehouse with grain (Deuteronomy 28:8). There's a big difference between spending everything you get and having a storehouse filled with grain.

At first it seemed impossible to get our ministry to a place where we were only using 30% of what came in. I decided, however, to work towards getting our ministry to that point, to follow Bishop Oyedepo's teaching. Once we started, we immediately noticed that God was blessing our efforts. Today we run our ministry at roughly less than 30% overhead, which allows us to stack up resources.

Are we hoarding? No, we're collecting the funds ahead of time. Hence, when the time comes to buy commercial property or do crusades, we won't have to beat $150,000 out of people because the money is due in 3 days. We have no debt. The money is stored up ahead of time for whatever move God wants us to make next.

Having a structure present allows God to increase you. The financial advisor for our ministry is on my Board of Directors. One time he told me that when he was praying, he felt like we should open up an account for stock donations. No one had ever offered to donate stock in the eight year history of our ministry. Yet, we moved forward with it. He prepared the paperwork and we simply had to sign in order to start receiving stock donations.

An hour after Magalis, our Executive Director, had signed the paperwork to receive stock donations, someone called from Queens, New York. He stated that he wanted to donate stock to our ministry. We made another vessel available for God to pour oil into. As soon as it was ready, someone used it to donate several thousand dollars of stock. Plan for increase; build a structure that God can bless.

Figure Out What You Are Called to Do

"I knew you before I formed you in your mother's womb. Before you were born I set you apart and appointed you as my prophet to the nations."

JEREMIAH 1:5

Jeremiah knew he was a prophet ordained from his mother's womb. Jeremiah knew the people and the work he was called to because God spoke to him. When an angel appeared to me in my room and said, "Jonathan, God has reserved you for this last period of time as an evangelist," I understood what God had called me to do. Thus, when I was offered a position as a youth pastor at two different churches, I didn't have to pray about it, I just said no. I knew my purpose was to be an evangelist, not a youth pastor.

Know what you're called to do. I'm not only talking about ministry, I'm talking about anything. If you're called to be a mechanic, what type of mechanic? The more you hone in on what you're called to do, the more productive you'll be.

Whom Am I Called to?

Paul was the apostle to the Gentiles. When he tried to preach to the Jews, he was an utter failure. Peter was called to the Jews, and he didn't have much success with the Gentiles. Not only do you need to know *what* you're called to do, but *whom* you're called to.

If you're in business, are you trying to reach poor people? Are you trying to reach middle-income people? Are you trying to reach high-income people? There's a big difference between getting a steak at the Golden Corral versus one at Ruth's Chris Steak House. Both restaurants are reaching two different markets. Ruth's Chris isn't trying to reach families with four kids, dressed in shorts and t-shirts, who want to consume three pounds of food apiece for a low price. They're only looking for high-end diners who have a couple of hours to lounge and eat. They want to keep you there so you can spend more money on appetizers, desserts, and wine. Golden Corral is making no effort to reach that population. They advertise for food at a low price. They know their target market.

Both restaurants know their target market. Likewise, you should know the demographic you're trying to reach in your own business.

Where Am I Called to Do It?

Jonah was a prophet so mightily anointed that he shook the whole city of Nineveh in a handful of days. Nevertheless, when he was on a ship headed in the wrong direction, he was more cursed than the heathen sailors with him. It's important that you are in the right place. God has a specific place for you. You need to know *where* you belong and complete what God has called you to do there.

I know people who used to have great ministries overseas. When they became fixated on wanting to preach in America, they lost their effectiveness and ended up with small meetings. The same thing happens with ministers who shake America and then decide to go overseas – they don't do nearly as well. Know where you're called to be.

Continually Access All Appropriate Knowledge

Appropriate knowledge means all knowledge that pertains to what God has called you to do. As a preacher, I've read countless books by powerful men of God. However, I don't just read books written by anyone. I've never read any books on how hard the ministry is or about a minister's struggle in the ministry. I locate successful people in my field and read everything they have. Their writings sharpen me. Hebrews 6:12 (NKJV) says, **"… Imitate those who through faith and patience inherit the promises [of God]."** By following them, I can read one book and absorb everything that took them 60 years to learn. To which afterwards, I can implement the same principles in my own ministry.

A friend of mine owns a construction business. He hit a wall at one point, with no new clients coming in. His income was slowing down and he was beginning to seem depressed. I felt led by the Holy Spirit to pay him a visit. When I stopped by, he was reading *The Gifts and Ministries of the Holy Spirit* by Dr. Lester Sumrall. I asked him what books he had on construction and he told me none. I explained to him that his business wasn't having a hard time because he was deficient in the gifts of the Spirit. He needed to read a book on how to increase his business. He needed to locate a book by someone who had success in his field, read how that person got clients, managed pricing, and so forth.

In my opinion, you should spend as much time reading or listening to materials pertaining to your business as you do, reading and listening to spiritual things. Today, information is more readily available than it's ever been. You can go on YouTube for free and watch videos of speakers that host seminars that cost hundreds or thousands of dollars to attend. There's never been an easier time to access information than right now. It's all at the tip of your fingers, and most of it is free.

Most people struggle because they don't cultivate their knowledge in the area to which God has called them. An accountant once studied his rich and poor clients and noticed a pattern. One of the things that separated his rich and poor clients was how they spent their time. For example, let's say people spend an hour a day in the car. Poor people use that time to listen to Top 40 music, sports radio, news-talk, and politics. Rich people use that time to listen to audiobooks and podcasts related to their business. If you want to be rich, copy what the rich do. They don't waste their time listening to nonsense, like debates on who the father is of a celebrity's baby.

Take that time and invest it in knowledge. Proverbs 11:9 says, **"With their words, the godless destroy their friends, but knowledge will rescue the righteous."** Knowledge is a rescue. The Bible says, my people are destroyed for lack of knowledge (Hosea 4:6). There are people that are destroyed, but it's not the devil destroying them. Their own lack of knowledge is destroying them. A lack of knowledge leads to captivity (Isaiah 5:13). People are being held captive in the prisons of poverty and sickness, and it's their own lack of knowledge keeping them there.

In Jesus' name, that will never be you! The same grace that drew you to this book is the grace that's going to cause you to pursue the knowledge of God. The knowledge and wisdom that God gives will cause you to do great things in life.

Chapter 9

Putting God in Remembrance of His Covenant

"Remember the LORD your God. He is the one who gives you power to be successful, in order to fulfill the covenant he confirmed to your ancestors with an oath."

DEUTERONOMY 8:18

I will never forget the day our ministry received $1 million dollars. I'll always remember the moment when the pastor gave us a note containing the offering total. My wife immediately took out her prayer book and flipped open to a note she wrote earlier that day: "Father you promised a 30, 60, or 100 fold return based on what we've given last year. On a 30 fold return, we are due $17 million. I would like the first million by today." That was her prayer and that night someone put $1 million dollars in the offering. Notice that Adalis didn't just claim to receive $1 million dollars because you won't find that principle in the Scriptures.

Adalis found in the Word where God said anyone that gives the seed produces – some 30, some 60, some 100 fold. She said, "God I know you're not a liar. We are due 17 million. I'd like the first million by tonight," and God answered her prayer. My wife's faith shocked me more than the money. I was glad I didn't hear her praying because if I had, I may have discouraged her. Even if I didn't say anything, I'd at least have thought, "That's a little ridiculous. We're at a church of under 200 people and she wants $1 million dollars tonight? I've never even heard of that happening."

1 John 5:14-15 (NKJV) says, **"Now this is the confidence that we have in Him, that if we ask anything according to His will, He hears us. And if we know that He hears us, whatever we ask, we know that we have the petitions that we have asked of Him."** My wife took God up on His Word and God didn't fail. There is a way to pray. The verse doesn't say, He might give us whatever we ask, it says, *He will give us whatever we ask.* There's a condition, however, that we must ask according to His will.

What does it mean to put God in remembrance of His covenant? You may surmise that since God wrote the Bible, putting Him in remembrance of His covenant is redundant. Believing that God doesn't need you to remind Him of what He said. Then again, Isaiah 43:26 (MEV) says, **"Put me in remembrance; let us plead together; state your cause, that you may be justified."** Like a lawyer, effective prayer makes a Scriptural case out of God's Word. It reminds Him of what He said, pleads that case, declares it, and receives its justification.

"'Present your case,' says the LORD. 'Bring forth your strong reasons,' says the King of Jacob."

Isaiah 41:21, NKJV

Effective prayer isn't defined by crying. Can you imagine if you had a lawyer in court and when it was time to present your defense, he started to cry? Imagine if he pleaded, "Your Honor, please, please don't. My client is such a nice person. They don't deserve to go to jail." If your lawyer spoke like that, you'd be finished. You might as well get the orange jumpsuit and handcuffs ready. How many Christians think prayer is simply pleading with God in tears? "Oh Lord, I've been going through this for so long. I don't have any money. I need your provision." That type of prayer isn't going to work.

The Bible says that God is moved to action through prayer. In Daniel 10, Daniel spent 21-days fasting and praying because he read Jeremiah's prophecy about how long the people of God were required to be in captivity in Babylon. He was burdened because the length of time had already passed and God's people were still in captivity. Daniel prayed and told the Lord, "You said in your Word that the time of our captivity was over, yet here we are still captive. I've done the math. We don't have to be in captivity anymore. I want an answer." On day 21, an angel came and said, "From the first day you prayed, I was sent with your answer. But for 21 days, the spirit prince of the kingdom of Persia held me up. But more angelic help was released and I've been sent with your answer." Making a case to God from the Word provokes answered prayer.

Bishop David Oyedepo once said that when he makes his prayer points, he always uses at least four Scriptures per point. When you pray, you should do the same. Pray like this: "Father you said this in your Word. I know you're not a man that you should lie, nor the son of man that you should change your mind. You said this, and it's true."

Although God said Israel would only be in captivity for a certain number of years, when that time expired, nothing happened. In order to bring Israel's captivity to an end, it took someone with knowledge about what God had promised – to pray and receive an answer. It was the same with the birth of Jesus. There wasn't only a prophecy that Jesus would be born, there were people like Anna who had studied and realized that it was time for the Messiah to be born. She ministered to the Lord with fasting and prayer saying, "I want to see the Messiah. Lord it's time for the Messiah to come, your Word says so. I don't want to die until I see Him." She knew when Jesus was born that He was the Messiah. She rejoiced because she received the answer to her prayer. Search the Word of God and locate Scriptures on what you're asking for.

My wife didn't simply say, "Oh God, please give us $1 million dollars." She made her case, "You said when we sow, that we are given 30, 60 or 100 return. I'm giving you the benefit of the doubt. I'm not asking for the 100 fold but your minimum of 30 fold. I have the numbers from our financial accounts of what we gave last year and we're due $17 million. I put in my request for it now, in accordance with your Word. I'd like the first million of that $17 million by tonight." God didn't get mad at Adalis for saying that prayer. On the contrary, He answered her prayer because the Bible says He delights in those types of prayers.

"Let us therefore come boldly to the throne of grace, that we may obtain mercy and find grace to help in time of need."

HEBREWS 4:16, NKJV

Don't pray like a beggar saying, "Oh God, I don't know what I'm going to do. Lord, if you could just please help me." That's not praying. Praying is finding what God said that's pertinent to your case and then presenting your case to the Lord.

In Oregon, a FM radio station started playing my programs twice a day. I attribute this to effectively engaging in prayer. I prayed and asked God, "Father, you said in 2 Peter 3:9 that you're not willing for any to perish, but you're giving more time for everyone to repent. You're waiting for more people to be saved. You *want* more people to be saved. I can help if you'll open more platforms for me to preach the gospel and for our program to go out. I ask you to do that right now, because you want it to happen. You said so in your Word. I remind you of that and I put in a request." Within 12 hours of saying that prayer, a radio station in Oregon contacted us. They said, "We've been watching your videos and we'd like to play your sermons on our radio show for free. We'll do the editing. We're just asking for the permission to broadcast it." Brothers and sisters, God isn't slow to answer prayer!

What does God's Word say on financial wealth? If you think the Bible is pro-poverty then your prayers won't help

139

expedite God's plan. Prayer isn't a substitute for sowing. Prayer isn't a substitute for giving. God has nothing good to say about poverty. The Bible talks about how the poverty of the poor is their destruction and the wealth of the rich is their safety (Proverbs 10:15).

Anyone in the Bible who came into contact with God and obeyed His commands, were blessed not cursed. The Bible guarantees your ability to live above need. God willed for there to be no poor Hebrew children as He led them into the Promised Land. Deuteronomy 15:4 says, **"There should be no poor among you, for the LORD your God will greatly bless you in the land he is giving you as a special possession."**

God has given us the ability to live above financial need:

"... The LORD is my shepherd, I lack nothing."

PSALMS 23:1, NIV

We have the ability to live about financial need. **"Not that I was ever in need..."** (Philippians 4:11). Put God in remembrance of His covenant. When He answered my wife's prayer and we received that $1 million dollars, she calmly showed the pastor her journal entry and said, "There will be much more where that came from." My wife's confidence is built in God's Word. She understands that she can take her case to God, and God will never deny His Word.

God has declared that we will lend only and never borrow:

Claim Deuteronomy 28:11 over your life when you're getting ready to make a move. The Bible says, the Lord will send rain at the proper time from his rich treasury in the heavens and will bless all the work you do. You will lend to many nations, but you will never need to borrow from them (Deuteronomy 28:11).

Pray this prayer: *"Father, I thank you that you're bringing me in this direction. I thank you that according to your Word, you said you'd cause me to lend only and never borrow. I thank you that there's a way to get this done where I'll never, ever have to go to a bank and fill out paperwork to try and convince some heathen to lend me money. You are my all-sufficient God. You are my Provider and you're going to take care of me."*

God has decreed an overflow of effortless wealth that will enable you to be a blessing:

"There was always enough flour and olive oil left in the containers, just as the LORD had promised through Elijah."

1 KINGS 17:16

God's Word declares an overflow of effortless wealth that enables you to be a blessing to your nation. God said four times in Galatians 3, that the same blessings and promises given to Abraham are given to all who put their faith in Jesus Christ. **"You prepare a feast for me in the presence of my enemies. You honor me by anointing my**

head with oil. My cup overflows with blessings" (Psalms 23:5).

Putting God in remembrance of His covenant applies to every area of your life. When you say, "Oh God, heal me. Oh God, I believe you're a healer" – that doesn't mean anything. Find scriptures in the Bible where God promised to give you vitality.

"…As your days, so shall your strength be."

DEUTERONOMY 33:25, NKJV

"Those who are planted in the house of the LORD shall flourish in the courts of our God. They shall still bear fruit in old age; they shall be fresh and flourishing."

PSALMS 92:13-14, NKJV

I can't reiterate enough the importance of studying God's Word and locating what the Bible says towards specific areas of your life. For example, 3 John 2:2 (NKJV) states, **"Beloved, I pray that you may prosper in all things and be in health, just as your soul prospers."** Locate what the Bible says on financial abundance and healing because those are two prongs the devil attacks most.

Next, locate what the Bible says about your mind being at peace, being able to sleep, and living free from anxiety. Find Scriptures like Isaiah 26:3 where it says, **"You will keep in perfect peace all who trust in you, all whose thoughts are fixed on you!"** Claim those Scriptures in prayer. Say, "Father I thank you that I never have to worry," and then present your case out of the Bible. Pray with boldness. Pray with expectation. Pray relentlessly, exercising your authority over the devil. Pray with thanksgiving. Use the name of Jesus. Pray from your heart, engage your spirit, and God will answer your prayer!

In contrast, don't use prayer for ways the Bible says you can't. For example, you can't pray your way out of poverty. You can quote all the scriptures you want to God, and yet if you sow nothing, there's no harvest promised to you. Once you've sown, pray this: *"Father, I thank you that whatever hand has been holding back my harvest, you cut it off today. You said you'd open the windows of heaven and pour out a blessing so great I'll never be able to take it all in. I thank you that nothing will hinder your ability to do so. I receive that today, in Jesus' name."*

The prayer of a righteous man has great power and produces wonderful results. It will be your fast track to a world of financial fortune (once you've been faithful in giving, which we covered earlier). Who knows what financial situation I'd be in today if my wife hadn't exercised her boldness in prayer? Her prayer produced results. Similarly, your prayer will produce results.

Pastor Adeboye, known as a man of prayer, petitioned God saying, "My prayer today, Lord Jesus, please make me what you want me to be. No more, no less, no shortcuts. Your own route." Let's pray that with the understanding it doesn't mean, "If you want me to be small, that's fine. If you want me to be someone that commands influence, that's fine." No, we know God has said, "I will bless you and make you great." We're telling Him we believe that plan, and we're asking Him to fulfill it.

Let me pray for you: *Lord Jesus, make those who are reading this what you want them to be – nothing more, nothing less. Like Abraham did with Ishmael, don't ever let them be tempted to take a shortcut. Show them your own path. Let them stick to that path and never deviate from it. I thank you for it. Anoint them afresh today. Use them to drive the devil out of this nation and the cities of this nation. Bring the people of America back to you. I pray that they'd not miss your will for their life by one step. Let them mark out a straight path for their feet on your route, and never take one step to the left or to the right. I give you all the praise, all the honor, and all the glory. In the mighty name of Jesus Christ, Amen.*

Chapter 10

Diligence

"Do you see a man diligent in business? He will stand before kings; he will not stand before obscure men."

PROVERBS 22:29, MEV

Diligence, in my opinion, is the principle that the Body of Christ fails most in upholding. Being diligent in what God has called you to is what will guarantee your rise to the top – where no one can stand in your way. When you're the best at what you do, no one cares about what you look like, the color of your skin, or your age. People will often say, "Nobody gives me a chance because I'm young... Nobody gives me a chance because I'm black... Nobody gives me a chance because I'm a woman." All that jargon flies out the window when you're the best at what you do.

Most Americans have heard the story of Jackie Robinson, the first African American baseball player allowed to play in Major League Baseball (MLB). The leagues were segregated at that time when the Dodgers signed Robinson, declaring the end of racial segregation in professional baseball. Do you think the Dodgers owner was any less racist than the owners of other MLB teams? They didn't sign Robinson to start a civil rights movement; they signed him because of his talent. They recognized that he was extremely talented at playing second base and the owner most likely thought, "I don't care about him being black because he's going to help me win. He's going to help me sell more tickets and as a result, make me more money." There's racism everywhere. There are racist National Football League (NFL) owners who would happily sign an all-black team if it would help them win.

Any time you hear people complaining about never getting and nothing ever opening up, it could be due to the fact that they lack excellence. If you're the best, no one cares about things others get hung up on. Someone might say, "They don't let me play drums at my church because the pastor's son plays." I'd beg to differ in that they'd allow you to play if you were a phenomenal drummer. The worship leader would speak to the pastor and say, "At the very least, please let this guy play drums on Wednesday and Sunday nights." Afterwards, when the rest of the congregation hears you play, people are going to start asking, "Why don't you have this guy play all the time? He's world-class."

Excuses are a crutch. The lazy man says, "Things aren't working out for me because I'm too young... I'm too old... I'm black... They don't like Spanish people." When you're the best, no one's going to remember what you look like. They'll primarily remember how excellent the product is that you produced.

How do you define diligence? Diligence is a ticket to the top. Diligence is not hard work. Diligence is hard, *excellent work.* I know absolutely nothing about fixing car engines. If I started a company to fix car engines, I might work hard all day and night. At the same time I'd constantly be frustrated trying to overcome one obstacle after another, day in and day out.

When customers call to check on their car three days later, it'd be in worse shape than they left it. I'd be out of business within two weeks once people realized I have no clue what I'm doing. Exasperated I'd say, "Man, I worked hard these two weeks. People don't care. They don't understand it takes a long time to fix a car engine." Although I might be working hard, I'm not excellent at what I do. Furthermore, it's not just hard work. It's hard, *excellent work.* If you're going to accomplish hard, excellent work in the field to which God has called you, three factors must be engaged: know your direction, know what it takes to get there, and do what it requires.

Know Your Direction

Where am I going? What am I called to do? As I mentioned in earlier chapters, the more specifically you know what God's called you to do, the better you'll be. It's not enough to know that I'm called into the ministry. When the angel spoke and decreed, "You are called to be an evangelist," I honed in on evangelism. I didn't dabble in pastoring. I didn't question becoming a youth pastor. I didn't say, "Well I guess I'll just become a pastor until my meetings pick up." I knew my direction and refused to go down any other path. If you don't know your direction, you'll quit. If things appear to be drying up or becoming tough, you'll find yourself saying, "Maybe I'm supposed to be doing something else." Get divine direction from God!

To be excellent, you must be convinced and fully persuaded as to what you're called to do. Otherwise, you'll be labeled as one of those people that go from one thing to another. During my travels, I come across people who seem to always be launching a new business idea. During conversation, they neglect to mention the business they launched two years ago. They simply move on to the next thing. Find your direction and stick with it.

If I told my wife to get in the car with me, the first question she would ask is, "Where are we going?" That's an intelligent question. The majority of people go through their entire life devoid of a defined direction. It's as if they get into the car of life and drive with no destination in mind – wherever you end up, you end up. Bishop David Oyedepo says, "If you don't know where you're going, anywhere looks like it."

When people don't know where they're heading, they end up anywhere. If Joseph never experienced his dream from God, (where the nations of the world would bow down to him) his interaction with Potiphar's wife may have been different. When she offered herself to him, even if he wasn't attracted to her, he might've been tempted to think, "If I marry her, I won't be a slave anymore. I'll be able to live in the house. I'll be owner of half this estate." However, Joseph knew his direction. He had already seen his end and knew it wasn't in Potiphar's house. Instead he could declare, "I've seen my end. The Lord has shown me what I'll be doing, before it's all said and done."

Know your direction. No one can decipher it for you, only God. Proverbs 3:6 (NKJV) says, **"In all your ways acknowledge Him, and He shall direct your paths."** Everything starts with divine direction.

Know What It Takes

Discovering what it takes is a paramount key in God causing the work of your hands to prosper. Be acquainted with what it takes for your business to be the best. Have knowledge of the direction you're going in. Identify what business, idea, or gift God has given you – then become aware of what it takes to accomplish.

Let me offer a few general examples of *what it takes*, that apply to anyone, no matter your career. Excellence should be demonstrated in everything that's connected to you. I'm amazed at how many people in ministry have completely out-of-date websites. If you click on their website calendar, you'll notice it hasn't been updated in months. If you click on the pastor's blog, you'll find one entry from three years ago. At the very least, take down the blog post you haven't been updating – it just looks bad. People take notice that you don't finish what you start.

When you click on their websites media tab a screen pops up – "coming soon." It's been "coming soon" for the last 18 months. If you ask whoever's in charge, their response is, "Ben our media guy said he's going to do it, but he hasn't done it yet. We've asked him to do it though." When people are viewing your uninspiring website, no one is thinking, "Oh, Ben just didn't do it yet." They're saying, "This church and pastor have a terrible website."

Ultimately, it reflects on you, the minister or business owner.

Don't allow any excuses for things to be left undone. If one of you said to a friend, "You have to come and hear this Jonathan Shuttlesworth guy," and they do a Google search on me – what comes up? If it's some low-grade video or audio, they'll most likely not be engaged in my ministry.

When people search for your company or business, their first impression is going to be based on what they find. That's why so many businesses pay companies to control what appears in their public Google search. If they come across a video of me speaking at a church that seats 6,500, along with a montage of clips in high-definition with professional audio, the person will automatically think – "This guy is a serious guy." If they're going to devote an hour and a half to listen to someone speak, they want it to be someone who appears to be worth their time. After all, who wants to spend an hour and a half listening to some clown talk?

The Bible says people judge by the outward appearance, but the Lord looks at the heart (1 Samuel 16:7). God is not your client. God is not your customer base, man is – and man judges by the outward appearance. Before Yelp was invented, all of us at some point, pulled into a restaurant without any prior knowledge of the establishment. You wanted to eat there because of the sign or building appearance. You judged the quality of food based on the graphics of the sign. There's no rhyme or reason to it, but that's what people do. Use that knowledge in your favor.

Do you have a website? If so, how does it look? If someone calls my ministry and invites us to preach at their church, we check their website. If one doesn't exist or is outdated, it lets me know that they aren't serious about the ministry, and most likely I decline the invite. It's not as if it's the year 1997 and the Internet just came out for public use. The internet has been available and easy to access for almost 20 years. The Internet is an incredible tool available to reach people. Not owning a website demonstrates that perhaps the leadership doesn't care. It may sound harsh, but we all make those judgments. I don't need to hear the pastor's heart or the church's vision. If they're doing a subpar job in the small things, I guarantee they're doing a subpar job in large things.

When people are diligent, everything looks good. There's a reason why certain people are at the top. People wrongly assume it's because they have a big staff and say, "If I had a large staff, my website and everything that represented me, would look nice too." That's not how it works. I guarantee that the people at the top were still doing things with excellence when they were small.

Years ago, when my wife handled everything for our ministry, our website was always up-to-date. We parted with 50% of our net worth to buy a camera so we could have professional pictures of our meetings. We didn't simply want to *tell* people what God was doing, but *show* people what God was doing. It's one thing for me to testify that we had 300 people come to the altar for salvation in a service. It's another thing to visually witness the pictures of people crying and being touched. We purchased the best camera and editing programs within our means. My wife enrolled in design courses online. If you believe you'll manage better when you have more money and resources, you're wrong. The effort you're putting in currently is the same amount of effort you'll put in when there's more money and resources available.

Correspondingly, that's how God promotes. God doesn't say, "I'll see how you do when you get more money. I understand you don't have much at your disposal right now." God says, as you're faithful in small things, He'll increase you and make you ruler over much (Matthew 25:21). Manage well, what you currently have in your possession. In addition to your website, think about your telephone. If you have a business is there a number for someone to call? What happens when someone calls that number? If it's your five year old child answering the phone saying, "Daddy's on the toilet right now," you're going to lose clients. There's a nominal fee to order a separate business line that rings to another phone. You can set up an automated voice answering system when you don't even own an office.

Anything you can acquire that offers excellence for the best price, do it – never compromise excellence to save money. There are many people who believe they're going to receive a crown in heaven for saving God money. Unfortunately for them, they're going to find out that God had plenty of money. He wasn't looking for people to save Him money. He was looking for excellence.

Web, phone, and marketing will be people's first introduction to you. Everything has to be marketed. Jesus separated his 72 disciples into groups of two. Jesus used marketing. There was no television, radio, or Internet; so Jesus sent his disciples ahead to announce he'd be coming to preach. Jesus didn't just roam around. He had a plan and an itinerary of the places he'd be visiting.

How are people going to find out about your business? You can produce the highest quality product there is, but if you sell it out of the trunk of your car and the only way for someone to find out about it, is to know your cousin – that's not excellence. If you craft beaded jewelry and your platform is the church lobby – that's not excellence. In fact, that's the antithesis of excellence. Have a way in which you're drawing consumers to your product. It's free to have a business Facebook page. You can run a targeted advertisement for a measly $5 dollars. Look into it. Don't just hope people find your business. Create a plan for how individuals are going to find your church, your business, etc.

There was a woman in Massachusetts that asked me to come and pray for her business. She couldn't figure out why she wasn't receiving any clients. I followed my GPS to the location of her business. Once I arrived at the address, I walked around for 45 minutes trying to find her business. Finally after a last ditch after, I walked into an abandoned-looking mall. There was only one store in the mall and it didn't even have a sign. I decided to check it out and sure enough, it was her business, a Christian bookstore. She said, "Jonathan, I don't understand why no one is coming here. Will you pray?" I said, "I will pray, but first you need to immediately order a sign. Even if people are looking for you, it's impossible to find your store."

I don't understand how Christians can be so ignorant when it comes to business and making money. It's not that difficult. Have a plan. Have a sign. Have marketing. Have a website. Have someone that answers your phone. Go ahead and run through that checklist right now. If anything isn't up-to-date: if you don't have a functioning phone, if your house is your business phone, if your cell phone is your business phone – you ought to take it seriously.

Seeking is an action you have to undertake, not God. If you want to do what's easy and take the low hanging fruit from the trees, you'll be poor. You'll have mid-level income your whole life. If you want to go to the top and come into the millions, tens of millions, and hundreds of millions – be diligent and excellent in everything you do.

Do What It Requires

In life, most people are aware of what's required of them to get where they want to be. Yet, they lack action. A minister can research how Billy Graham or Oral Roberts established impactful and successful ministries. In spite of this, even if some ministers discovered the information and were given the steps to take their ministry to the next level, they won't do it. They're neither interested nor invested enough to actually put in the work that's required.

Do what it requires and make a covenant with God. Say this, *"God, I'm all in with what you've given me. I'm going to carry out what you've shown me to fulfill with all my might. Whatever it costs, I will pay it. I'm not working six hour days, four days a week – I'm all in. I yield my life for the task you've assigned me. I'm going to build it. I'm going to make it excellent."*

"Last of all, as though I had been born at the wrong time, I also saw him. For I am the least of all the apostles. In fact, I'm not even worthy to be called an apostle after the way I persecuted God's church. But whatever I am now, it is all because God poured out his special favor on me – and not without results. For I have worked harder than any of the other apostles; yet it was not I but God who was working through me by his grace."

1 CORINTHIANS 15:8-10

After they stoned Paul, he didn't take a three-week sabbatical. He got up from the rubble, walked to his next meeting, and continued to preach. That's what you call *all in*. When you read the account of his story, depicting the several times he was lashed, beaten with rods, shipwrecked at sea and all the more – none of that stopped him from fulfilling God's purpose for his life.

Don't be lazy. Don't feel sorry for yourself. Don't allow the words, "I'm tired," to come out of your mouth. Be strong in the Lord and in the power of His might. Move in the direction God has given you. Work tirelessly and be the best at what you do. Be diligent. Be fully committed to what God has beckoned you to complete. Engage the three principles regarding diligence: know your direction, know what it takes to get there, and commit to what it requires – and you'll go to the top, in Jesus' mighty name.